The Pleasure of God

The Pleasure of God

Finding Grace in the Ordinary

J. ELLSWORTH KALAS

WESTMINSTER
JOHN KNOX PRESS
LOUISVILLE · KENTUCKY

First edition
Published by Westminster John Knox Press
Louisville, Kentucky

16 17 18 19 20 21 22 23 24 25—10 9 8 7 6 5 4 3 2 1

Book design by Drew Stevens
Cover design by Allison Taylor

Library of Congress Cataloging-in-Publication Data
Kalas, J. Ellsworth, 1923-
  The pleasure of God : finding grace in the ordinary / J. Ellsworth Kalas. — First edition.
    pages cm
  ISBN 978-0-664-26118-4 (alk. paper)
1. Christian life. I. Title.
  BV4501.3.K353 2016
  248.4—dc23

                                            2015027961

♾ The paper used in this publication meets the minimum requirements of the American National Standard for Information Sciences—Permanence of Paper for Printed Library Materials, ANSI Z39.48-1992.

Most Westminster John Knox Press books are available at special quantity discounts when purchased in bulk by corporations, organizations, and special-interest groups. For more information, please e-mail SpecialSales@wjkbooks.com.

CONTENTS

CHAPTER 1

THE PLEASURE OF GOD:
A WAY OF LIFE

For some years before the followers of Jesus were called Christians, they were known as "the people of the Way." This was true both within the community of believers and among those who opposed and persecuted them. Even after the author of the book of Acts says that "they were first called Christians at Antioch," he continues to refer to the believers by what was obviously the most common title at the time: "people of the Way." Many biblical translations now capitalize *Way* to indicate that it is indeed a name and not just a description.

Nevertheless, one of the loveliest things about this name is that it is also a description. It reminds us that when Jesus called disciples, it was with the simple, straightforward invitation, "Follow me." This infers a commitment that results in an action and then in a way of life. The first believers knew that to join this company of Jesus was more than affiliating with an organization and more even than accepting a body of beliefs—what we today call doctrines.

Indeed, at that time, the doctrinal verities were still being spelled out in the teaching of the apostles and recorded in apostolic letters, especially those by Paul. Those persons who made up the company of believers after the crucifixion and resurrection had heard a call to follow — not in the physical fashion of the original disciples, who left homes and jobs to accompany Jesus on his travels, but with the same deep sense of reality and decision. And they knew that in following Jesus they were choosing not only a Savior and a belief but something utterly different from the myriad of religions and philosophies that were then being practiced in the Roman Empire and beyond. They were choosing a way of life.

This way of life was not an escape from the world but a way of living within it. It affirmed the world as a residence, though not the end of it all. It insisted that this world was a place of divine purpose and that those who chose this way were declaring their commitment to bring that purpose to pass. The prayer that Jesus gave his followers declared as much. The prayer was short, down to earth, and very much to the point. After identifying God as Father in heaven and hallowing the name, the prayer moved to petitions — particularly, and before anything else, that God's kingdom should come and God's will be done on earth as in heaven. And lest one think that the prayer had to do with matters particularly heavenly, it moved immediately to the most basic of matters: a petition for daily bread. Then it included an appeal that God would forgive our sins, just as we would forgive others. This request is as essential to our spiritual and emotional health as bread is to our physical existence, because it deals with our three basic relationships with: God, our fellow humans, and our own souls. The final petition is a basic matter of daily life: an appeal for God's help in resisting temptation. After all, if we give in to temptation, we'll lose the Way.

This Way leads to heaven, an eternal reunion of humanity with our Creator and Lord. But it has much more to say
about our relatively short journey on this earth than about
eternity in heaven. Sometimes the earnest preacher or
believer asks, "Suppose I die tomorrow—what then?" Here's
a better question: "Suppose I live tomorrow—what then?"

I'm not playing down eternity. Quite the opposite;
I'm saying that this life today is of a piece with eternity.
When a clergyman came to visit Henry David Thoreau in
the last days of Thoreau's life and asked if there was any
sense of what followed, Thoreau answered memorably,
"One world at a time." Our first-century faith ancestors
didn't distinguish the two worlds so sharply; they made
themselves ready for the world to come by living with a
grand sense of God's presence and purposes in this present world. This was part of the way Jesus contrasted
himself with the false shepherds: "The thief comes only
to steal and kill and destroy. I came that they may have
life, and have it abundantly" (John 10:10). The abundance Christ promised begins here—not in the measure
of land possessed or honors won, but in those measures
that are appropriate to creatures such as you and me,
people blessed with the breath of eternity in our persons
and spirits.

This brings us to the matter of the kind of people we
are. Whatever might be said of our moments of ecstasy,
profundity, or nobility, or those rare occasions when individuals seem to shape history, most of our time, whoever
we are, is spent in common stuff. It's easy to find the statistics about how we spend our time to be somewhat dispirit-
ing. We spend fully a third of our lives sleeping. It's even
more than that during infancy and early childhood, but we
spend nearly as much time in our adult lives sleeping or
trying to sleep. And about work: the standard in America
is the forty-hour workweek. But an increasing percentage
of people are working more (sometimes much more) than

forty hours a week, some because they love the work they do and some because they need overtime or a second job in order to meet their financial obligations.

And then there's more of the common stuff: eating or preparing food, or waiting for it in a restaurant or in our cars outside a fast-food establishment; waiting for traffic to move; standing in line at a checkout counter or for admission to an entertainment or sporting event; bathing, brushing and flossing teeth, shaving, caring for hair or the lack thereof, dressing, and making decisions about what to wear. And, of course, there are the elephants in the room of time consumption: television, the Internet, and the ubiquitous phone that is almost an extension of the hand if not the ear. So it is that our sixty, seventy, eighty, ninety years go by in common ways, and we hardly know where they've gone.

Is there a glory in all of this? Is this all there is to life? Where is the abundance of which Jesus spoke? Where is there greatness in the commonness of most of life?

There is a beautiful line in *Chariots of Fire,* a movie that won a host of awards in 1981 and 1982. The movie was based on events surrounding the 1924 Olympics, particularly involving two admirable figures. Harold Abrahams hoped to make a statement for his people, the Jews, and Eric Liddell planned to be a missionary to China like his parents. (The real Liddell did, in fact, die there in 1945 for his faith as a prisoner of war.)

Early in the story, Liddell's sister, Jenny, worries that her brother is putting his running ahead of his calling as a missionary. Liddell assures his sister that he is as committed as ever to his missionary vocation and then continues, "I believe that God made me for a purpose. But he also made me *fast,* and when I run I feel his pleasure."

The line was probably written by the screenwriter, as it doesn't appear in Liddell's biography. But it gets to the point of Eric Liddell's life. As Catherine Swift says in her biography, Liddell's faith was something "he had lived . . . all his life. It was as natural as eating, bathing, sleeping, and breathing."[1]

This is the way of saints, who find the stuff of life in its common hours. How else, when most of our hours are common? I cherish daily prayers, daily Bible reading, and using my time and resources in the service of Christ. As a pastor and teacher, I have encouraged others to practice such disciplines as well. But I'm uneasy with measuring Christianity by statistics as we do with sports, business, and politics. We must not tally verses read as we do home runs or contracts signed. Saints are not those who offer many prayers, but those who turn all of life into a prayer.

G. K. Chesterton, that remarkable Catholic journalist, critic, novelist, and man-about-town, put it well:

> You say grace before meals.
> All right.
> But I say grace before the play and the opera,
> And grace before I open a book,
> And grace before sketching, painting,
> Swimming, fencing, boxing, walking, playing, dancing,
> And grace before I dip the pen in the ink.[2]

The saint is someone who whether walking, eating, resting, emailing, laughing, or socializing does it with such gladness of soul as to say, "God made me thus, and when I so live, *I feel his pleasure.*" It follows that anything which cannot be lived with such holy gladness should not be part of one's life.

Does it seem presumptuous, indeed arrogant, to think that what we do with our ordinary lives might give pleasure to God? To the contrary, it adds beauty to the love of God that God would be so attentive as to care about our daily lives.

And it redefines *ordinary*. How can anything be ordinary if we find the glory of God there? How so, if in it we feel God's pleasure?

DAILY PROMISE

Today I will see the uncommon potential in all the ordinary elements of this day. I intend to feel God's pleasure in all that I do.

CHAPTER 2

EATING

Our culture sees eating as one of life's secular activities. On the most basic level, eating is necessary for survival. It's the crumb of bread or the handful of rice that keeps us alive. Nevertheless, it is also the key element of those occasions when we want to celebrate. Whether it is coffee and a pastry with a friend, hors d'oeuvres at a reception, or cake at a birthday or wedding, food is the essence of celebration. Yet it is so much the stuff of daily life that we measure it statistically: number of calories consumed, cost plus tip for the server, how many to be invited for dinner, or the amount we can save by clipping coupons from the Sunday paper.

At least once a year, at Thanksgiving, even our secular culture acknowledges God's relationship to food. So, too at those public dinners a formal prayer is deemed proper. Much of the time, however, the attitude of our world about God and mealtime is conveyed in the mood of the iconic Norman Rockwell painting of a grandmother and grandson with heads bowed in a New England diner, while those at nearby tables look on with expressions that convey embarrassment, curiosity, and admiration.

The Bible sees eating as the good gift of God, one of the favors by which the Creator has blessed his creation.

Jesus enjoyed eating, and others enjoyed eating with him. His enemies accused him of being a winebibber and a glutton. We have no evidence that he was ever intoxicated or that he was guilty of overeating. Perhaps his enemies attached those labels out of jealousy of his popularity, but I wonder if it is also because they envied the obvious pleasure Jesus found at the table. For him, eating was more than a means of staying alive and more even than a conventional opportunity for celebration; it was part of the pleasure of meeting in the presence of the Father. To fast for forty days not only cut our Lord off from daily sustenance but also took away the joy associated with eating.

A seriously abstemious soul might remind me that it was by eating that our spiritual ancestors in Eden got into trouble and that when our race got a second chance via Noah, Noah himself upset things again by overdrinking. Obviously, there's a point to be made. At the least, it shows our inclination to pervert life's loveliest favors so that they become instruments of destruction—of both ourselves and others.

But see how the Bible portrays food as a gift of God, not only for sustenance and necessity but also for celebration. "See," God says, "I have given you every plant yielding seed that is upon the face of all the earth, and every tree with seed in its fruit; you shall have them for food" (Gen. 1:29). The presence of seed within the plant and its fruit tells us that the system is structured to continue replicating itself for as long as we cooperate with its doing so. The variety of these fruits and plants is probably beyond our numbering, and I venture that we will keep adding to the list as we continue discovering the wealth of our creation. It's appropriate that this sentence about food is the last word of the creation story, other than the Creator's obvious pleasure in the perfection of the finished product. Then comes the first Sabbath, a day of rest and celebration.

The biblical drama takes its sharpest turn in the call of Abraham and Sarah, so all that follows, including the New Testament story, unfolds from that call. When the story seems close to a morass, an angelic team visits Abraham and Sarah by the oaks of Mamre. In classic understatement, Abraham asks, "Let me bring a little bread, that you may refresh yourselves." By "little bread" he really means "choice flour," "a calf, tender and good," and "curds and milk," which his guests eat while Abraham stands at a tree nearby as if he were the waiter in a restaurant whose solitary obligation was to watch over one table (Gen. 18:1–8). It is in this setting that God confides to Abraham a message of miracle and of judgment. The Genesis writer makes clear that the meal provides the setting for such a discussion. Every business luncheon since has been a fumbling imitation of that hour.

The story of Israel's years in the wilderness is a spiritual idyll with one continuing motif: daily bread. Manna. The same every morning, yet new every morning. Certainty, but no surprises. Adequate, but predictable. For many of us, all our meals become like manna: there, predictable, meeting our needs, but without a true sense of celebration. So it is with the stomach that receives the food. The specialist knows that the stomach is a wonderfully intricate machine, but it is only fully appreciated when it fails to function in its taken-for-granted way. Otherwise, the stomach seems quite ordinary.

The Old Testament calendar insisted on more. There were special days in the Hebrew calendar; all of them were religious days, and all but one were feast days. The inference was clear for those who would see it. God found pleasure in the feasting of his people. As one who has been privileged to live in several cities with a sizable Jewish population, I submit that the Jewish delicatessen is a vestigial reminder that God's people find pleasure in eating. The spiritual quality may no longer be prominent, but the taste and the serving size are physical evidence of a holy joy.

So Jesus ate. He showed his divinity in the midst of his humanity. He ate with publicans and sinners, who by practice were a raucous crowd. His disciples plucked and ate grain as they walked on the Sabbath, to the distress of strict religious legalists. Jesus ate at the home of his dear friends Martha, Mary, and Lazarus. When a crowd stayed long while listening to his teaching, Jesus told his disciples, "Give them something to eat." He made a miracle of the meal, with such abundance that there were twelve baskets of leftovers. God's pleasure at that mealtime was opulent. As for the day when our world will stand at Jesus' judgment seat, Jesus said that a key test will be this: "I was hungry, and you gave me food to eat," or "I was hungry, and you gave me no food" (Matt. 25:35–42). That seems a very pragmatic standard of judgment and not an obviously pious one unless we believe that God not only wants our spiritual needs to be supplied but also finds pleasure in the satisfying of our most elementary (and alimentary) needs.

So how ought we to eat? Certainly, to recognize that food is one of the few utter essentials of life. If God prizes our continued existence, then food is essential, and God finds pleasure at the least in our survival. But the variety God has provided seems also to say that God has built aesthetics into food. What is so beautiful as a tomato bursting with ripeness in a backyard garden, or a melon cleaved for sale in a super-market? Such beauty should be eaten with care.

There also should be emotion with food. "Bread I broke with you," the poet says in sad reminiscing, "was more than bread."[1] Nehemiah was a tough-minded preacher-administrator, but he also had a proper theology of food. As he called for a return to God, he interrupted the people's mourning and weeping. "Go, eat rich food, and drink something sweet" (Neh. 8:9–10), he admonished the people. Enjoy!

And give food proper attention. It's blasphemous to shovel in food as if we were stoking a furnace. We eat less when we taste more. Joshua Sundquist remembers a day when he was settling in, as was his custom, to multitask, eating a favorite salad while handling email and telephone messages. Then he realized that though he was eating his salad, he wasn't tasting it—not the lime dressing, not the chicken, not the tasty parmesan.[2]

To eat in God's presence is also to eat with a conscience. The supreme wickedness of a certain rich man was that "he feasted sumptuously every day" while a beggar neighbor longed for a few crumbs (Luke 16:19–31). If table graces throughout the centuries remind us to be mindful of those who have not, instead of settling for the words, we should receive an offering for a poverty food program as soon as the meal is completed—even if it is simply a family gathering.

And we should know how to rejoice in what we have. That remarkable sixteenth-century nun Teresa of Avila one day received a partridge from a generous friend. As she was eating it with pleasure, someone reprimanded her. Teresa replied, "There is a time for partridge and a time for penance."[3]

If we eat as God would have us eat, God will find pleasure in our eating. The Giver will rejoice in the good taste of the receiver.

DAILY PROMISE

Today I will treat my eating as a sacrament.
Whether alone or in a noisy public place, whether
the usual fare or something out of the ordinary,
I will savor it with uncommon appreciation.

CHAPTER 3

SLEEPING

We spend at least a third of our lives sleeping—or trying to sleep, or trying to stay awake when sleepiness becomes insistent at inappropriate times. In the earliest years of our lives, we spend a good deal more than a third, and some who live to advanced ages return to a more extended pattern of sleep as they age. Sleep experts say that many adults are sleep deprived and that we are suffering from this deprivation physically, mentally, and emotionally. We need at least seven hours a night, they say, and still better eight—that is, a third of each day.

If the importance of what we do is measured best by the time we give to it, then sleeping is our most important activity—or *inactivity*, if you please—since not only do we give it a substantial part of our time, but we do so every day, except for rare occasions or if we are extraordinary persons.

Our faith ancestors knew how to go to sleep. They did it with prayer. There was a children's prayer that many carried into their adult lives. It was a kind of insurance policy for the night, renewable every evening, preferably on one's knees:

Now I lay me down to sleep;
I pray Thee, Lord, my soul to keep.
If I should die before I wake,
I pray Thee, Lord, my soul to take.

It's a prayer with a long, long history. It was included in the *New England Primer* in the 1690s, but our first record of it goes back to 1160, in the *Enchiridion Leonis*. And who knows what prior history it may have had.

We moderns and postmoderns are uneasy with such a regular reminder that we are mortal and that it's possible we will prove it before the night is over. Our ancestors lived closer to death than most of us do because death usually happened in the home rather than in a hospital or some other special institution. Perhaps they were also more sensitive to the similarity between sleep and death. Jesus gave this similarity a lovely hue when he said of both Jairus's daughter and Lazarus that they were not dead but sleeping.

Whether or not we like the idea of going to sleep thinking we might not awaken, it seems likely that on the whole our ancestors slept better than we do. Statistics are risky business, but the best available say that in a recent year, Americans spent $32 billion on sleep-related medicine and counsel and that this expenditure has gone up an average of 8.8 percent every year since 2012.

Does it matter to God whether we sleep well, or poorly, or not at all? The psalmist thought so: "I lie down and sleep; / I wake again, for the Lord sustains me." Tradition says that David wrote those words when he was fleeing for his life from a revolt led by his son Absalom. He declared that he was "not afraid of ten thousands of people / who have set themselves against me all around" (Ps. 3:5–6). That's the kind of situation where even a hardy soul would feel justified in reaching for some sort of medical escape hatch. Sleeping aids existed in David's time, although not in the variety available to us or as attainable. Yet David slept—"for the Lord sustains me." And he did this not only when his life was in danger but also at a time of excruciating personal anguish: His own son—perhaps the most notable and appealing—had turned against him, and with him many of David's most trusted personal and administrative associates. Still, David *slept*.

Perhaps our ancestors had an edge on us in one respect. Except for a very wealthy few, their way of life was far more physical than ours. Most labor was physical labor, and they got to their place of work by physical means. Our work is more often sedentary, and it tends often to be the kind of work that claims our attention even after we have left our workplaces. That is, much of our work cooperates with our worry-urge. But we can't fully excuse ourselves. David had something to worry about with "ten thousands . . . having set themselves against me all around."

And if it's worry that keeps one from sleeping, think of the prophet Elijah. When he heard that Queen Jezebel had vowed to find him and kill him, he fled for his life. Then, somewhat ironically, he asked God if he might die. Instead, however, he lay down under a broom tree and fell asleep. It's as if God said, "You're not dead. Just sleeping." God awakened him with a fresh cake and a jar of water. Elijah ate and then slept again until once more God awakened him. It's clear that Elijah had worries enough to keep him awake, but he slept.

While Elijah and David experienced the blessing of sleep as God's provision, and David witnessed to it in a song of thanksgiving, Solomon, in one of two psalms credited to him, claims sleep as a blessing available to all of God's children. He reminds us, in the style of the wisdom literature we associate with his name, that "unless the Lord builds the house, / those who build it labor in vain," and so too with those who guard a city (Ps. 127:1). Then he makes a statement that is quite unlikely for a wise man:

It is in vain that you rise up early,
and go late to rest,
eating the bread of anxious toil;
for [God] gives sleep to his beloved.
(Ps. 127:2)

Some Bibles give a footnote with an alternate translation: "for he provides for his beloved during sleep." It sounds as if the biblical writer—and in this instance, one who is known for his wisdom—is endorsing laziness: Don't waste your life getting up early and going to bed late. God loves you and will bless you while you're sleeping.

But this is not necessarily a flight from reason. Rather, it may be wisdom that we've too often overlooked. I've heard from people as diverse (or not) as poets and garage mechanics who are trying to figure out how to solve a work problem—the right repair to a motor or the right repair to a broken line of words—only to awaken in the morning, or even in the middle of the night, with the solution clear and ready in their minds. They needed to be done with the worries that were in the way of productive thinking and to be free from a dead end so that their refreshed minds could receive the solution they'd been missing all along. It reminds me of a story from the legendary Bishop William Alfred Quayle. Worried about the churches and ministers under his leadership, he tossed sleeplessly for an hour and more until God said to him, "Bill, you go to sleep, and I'll stay up and worry the rest of the night." The theology of the story may be suspect, but a lesson is clear: if we were better listeners, some nights we might hear the same message from God.

I have no medical credentials, nor am I a sleep specialist. But while sleeplessness is a physical fact, often with distinct physical problems, it is also to some extent a matter of attitudes. Some of these attitudes are woven into us so deeply that only a mental or emotional explosion could break us free from them. But we could help by opening ourselves to such an inner revolution. It isn't the business of this book, however, except perhaps by extension.

Our issue is the pleasure of God and how we might give pleasure to a loving God by the common practices of our common lives. Might God find pleasure in our sleep? David obviously thought so, when the distresses of his life and his failures as a father piled on him during as dark a night as one might imagine. And Solomon thought so as he pondered the futility of some of humanity's best, most earnest labors.

But of course! If a parent or grandparent or babysitter can look at a sleeping infant with pleasure beyond phrasing, would not our Lord so see us? Sleep is the ultimate act of trust. We enter it only by giving up control (and perhaps this is why we find it so difficult to do). The ancient prayer is quite right: we never know what might happen while we sleep, what intruder might enter not simply our house but our mind, our spirit, our unprotected soul. To sleep is the most common act of faith exercised by our human race, regardless of our degree or sense of religion. It is our unconscious act of trust in Someone, whether or not we acknowledge that Someone.

Of course, that Someone smiles when we sleep. And if in our sleeping we consciously entrust our bodies and minds and souls to our Lord, I'm very certain that our sleep gives him pleasure.

Good night.

DAILY PROMISE

Tonight I will remind myself that God created rest and will trustingly rest assured that God finds pleasure in my proper use of the gift of sleep.

CHAPTER 4

BATHING

The Scriptures tell us in one way and another that bathing has holy implications. I learned this truth before I understood that much Scripture. I got it by way of the Saturday night bath.

Yes, Virginia, there was a Saturday night bath. The concept wasn't invented by novelists or discovered by an anthropologist researching the practices of some remote people. It was the way of life of my boyhood in Iowa, and I dare to imagine that it is still part of the religious ritual in various places not only in the United States but in places in Africa or South America.

One took a bath on Saturday night not because one needed it then more than, say, midweek but because one was going to Sunday school and church the next morning. One also polished one's shoes on Saturday night, and someone in the family—most likely mother or older sister—mended clothes that would be worn to church. We did this because going to church was very special. One should be at one's best when coming to the house of God.

Why didn't we bathe every day? Because water and soap cost money, but especially because hot water was hard to come by. We lived in the city and had running water, but like a substantial percentage of people in those Depression years, we had only one variety of water: cold. And heating it for a bath was expensive and difficult, especially if the whole family bathed.

When I became a student in junior high school, with gym classes twice a week, I learned that cleanliness was also nice on Tuesdays and Thursdays. But that didn't change the Saturday night ritual. The polished shoes, the mended clothes, and the scrubbed body were matters of practiced reverence. We intended to be at our human best before God.

A worldly wise cynical voice interrupts me: "You were trying to impress other people." Perhaps at times, in some measure. Only the greatest saints do goodness with utterly unmixed motives, and even for them, not always. But primarily, insistently, we reminded ourselves that we were paying honor to God by our extra effort of cleanliness. That's how I learned that God finds pleasure in my bathing. And in some measure, I've never gotten over it.

Only later did I learn that the Jews knew this several thousand years ago. The ordination of Aaron and his sons began at the entrance to the tent of worship, where Moses washed them with water before clothing them in the special garments of their office (Exod. 29:4). I hardly need say that the washing symbolized a cleansing beyond the body. Each time Israel's priests came to minister, they were to wash their hands and their feet (Exod. 30:17–21).

The basic principle extended to the whole community of Israel. Certain bodily conditions or acts were seen as "unclean," so there were explicit instructions for washing and bathing (Lev. 15). The Jews were a notably clean people and lived by strict rules of cleanliness in a world where water was often in short supply and where it was acquired by effort. The only running water was in a spring or a river. Israel's apparently careless use of water must have mystified its neighboring nations. But Israel's priests bathed out of respect for their holy office and its functions, and the people bathed to remind themselves that they were a holy people. In the process, Israel practiced sanitation in a fashion that was still not common in the Western world until into the nineteenth century.

The symbolic significance of bathing got a dramatic touch in the story of Naaman. He was a great Syrian general, honored by his king and his people, but in time afflicted with leprosy. In those days, the term *leprosy* covered a wide range of skin disorders but always induced the fear of contagion and possible disfigurement and disablement. A Jewish slave girl in Naaman's household urged Naaman to seek help from the prophet Elisha. When Naaman did so, Elisha rather peremptorily sent him to bathe seven times in the Jordan River. At first, Naaman protested that he had better rivers back in Syria, until one of his servants urged a more reasonable response. The story is partly a lesson in faith and in obedience, but it also is a lesson in the significance of bathing as a faith ritual.

In fact, bathing is so fit a religious symbol that one wonders how long it has been part of every faith practice. We humans discovered that it was pleasant to feel clean after feeling dirty. How long did it take humans to feel unclean after an immoral or distasteful act and then to ponder a ritual that would associate with the sense of inner cleanliness? Some ritual that might either aid in the sense of moral cleansing or that would provide a means of celebration after inner cleansing had occurred? The term *baptism* seems to belong to the church, but the idea of physical and spiritual cleansing is inevitably linked in the human mind. Pilate wasn't an advocate of John the Baptist when at Jesus' trial he took water and washed his hands before the crowd, declaring, "I am innocent of this man's blood" (Matt. 27:24). Pilate could have spoken the words without the act, but something about the act of physical cleansing spoke to his soul. It is instructive that we have carried this picture into our common conversation so that under certain circumstances we say, "I'm washing my hands of this whole affair." Anything that is for some reason distasteful, from which we want to free ourselves, calls for a cleansing, a washing, a bathing.

Life is a process in which we repeatedly get soiled and need to be cleansed. This is physically true, as all of us know. We live in a germ-conscious age, but even without that pressure we say, "I don't know why I feel dirty. I haven't worked that hard. But I need to wash my hands." Of course. We live in air that has qualities of impurity, and we live in bodies that excrete—even those of us who think ourselves too delicate to perspire. Just as surely, the human soul deals hourly with that which soils the soul and spirit and with thoughts, often unbidden, that have the same dirtying effect. We need to bathe.

If you've forgotten the glory of washing your face or taking a shower, attend the ritual of bathing an infant. When the ritual is complete, see how wonderful is the tousled head of hair, the laughter as the act reaches a certain point where the mother or father or sibling or grandparent crowns the clean baby with a kiss. Or listen to someone who has lived in a detainment or military prison camp, where such cleansing was rare or even nonexistent. They can tell you that water is essential first for drinking, then for bathing.

Many years ago I made a case for another kind of bathing. I was pastor of a downtown church where men and sometimes women came to us off the street, dirty and diminished of their worth. Part of our task as a church was to do all that we could and all that the persons would allow to bring them to inner cleansing, to redeeming faith. But I knew that they also needed the simple physical act of bathing, so I made a case for showers in the new building we were planning. I moved to another church before our building plans were complete, and my appeal was lost in the process, but if I had such a chance again, I would make the same case.

It's really not surprising that singing in the shower or the bathtub has become iconic. We smile about the persons whose inability to carry a tune means that they should restrict their singing to such a place of privacy, but our humor testifies to the profound human significance of bathing. Some bathe in the evening, to be cleansed for sleep, while others bathe in the morning, to be empowered for the day. I happen to belong to the first group, but in a sense I enjoy both worlds. For me, shaving in the morning completes what began the night before with bathing. I love the peculiar cleanness that comes when I remove that layer of skin and stubble. I find that almost inevitably I am humming a tune of some favorite, long-forgotten song. So I sing in the shower and hum while shaving.

Many of the hymns of my childhood (for which I thank God) were songs of religious experience, and they spoke often of cleansing and forgiveness. They recognized that we humans know that we get soiled by life—sometimes desperately so. We need to be washed.

It is a proper attitude to take into the bath or shower, whether at night or in the morning, that we are being cleansed of the stuff of the day—not because it is necessarily bad of itself (though surely some of it is) but because we need the *clean* feeling. We need to know that God finds pleasure in our bathing, our cleansing, with its holy freshness for better living.

DAILY PROMISE

Today I will see my bathing as an internal, spiritual
cleansing as well as an external, physical one.
I will see my bathed body as a fresh start.

CHAPTER 5

COMMUTING

Commuting is a relatively modern invention. Few products of modernity are more in need of redemption. Moving itself is not a problem; we humans have always been movers. The writer of Genesis shows us on the move as Adam and Eve leave Eden, and we never get over it. The inhabitants of Babel wanted to stay where they were, and God moved them on. The Bible describes Abraham as a friend of God, and God celebrated the friendship by telling him, "Go from your country and your kindred and your father's house to the land that I will show you" (Gen. 12:1). Some move to escape, some to start again, some because of boredom, and some for reasons they know not. Most of us move, but moving is not commuting.

Commuting happens to people who have already moved. Commuting is one of the unexpected results of progress. Few, if any, would call it a benefit. It's the price of living in an urban culture, where business occupies so much territory and where business is big enough that there's not room for many people to live where their livelihood is. This is different from the age-old agricultural economy, where people lived with their work, and different also from the world of household manufacturing or of businesses where people lived above the store or the shop.

Then came the commuter train, making it possible to live some distance from one's work; then better still, the automobile. The automobile did it so well that people began to live still farther from their work. Millions have come to do this in a peculiarly perverse fashion, so that people who work on the West Side live on the East Side and every day can pass their commuting West Side equivalents who work on the East Side.

Metropolitan areas now vie for the title of city with the most time commuting to work. As I write this, Atlanta holds the record, but New York, Los Angeles, and Boston are also in the running. Commuting is expensive, but many commute because even with the cost of transportation, they save money by avoiding the cost of living, of housing, or of taxes in the city of their work. But the highest cost of commuting is its toll on the body, family, or community life, and the increased sense of pressure and strain. For some, the commute is weekly rather than daily because home is in the Midwest and work is on one coast or the other. Some commute weekly from Atlantic to Pacific, expecting to do so for only part of a year, while others contract for several years of such a life.

Can the twenty-first-century commuter who is caught in traffic say from a full soul, "As I navigate this highway, I feel God's pleasure"? Brother Lawrence found God's pleasure in the pots and pans of the monastery kitchen; indeed, he felt it as much as he did in celebrating the sacrament. But he could remind himself that he was tending the kitchen in a consecrated place; it's harder to baptize the crush of life on the interstate.

I don't think Brother Lawrence would let us off that easily. If we believe that God is in life from the sparrow's fall to the whirlwind out of which God spoke to Job, we can't exclude the airport concourse or the run for the commuter train from the realm of God's pleasure—not if all of life is God's domain and if God seeks to be with us in all of life.

Some hope that God will find pleasure in their efficiency, their ability to multitask. If one can travel to or from work and at the same time do some work, this must be at least as good as Brother Lawrence's well-scrubbed pans. If time is sacred, as many of us believe, then to use it rather than waste it is an act of holiness. Paul tells us that those who are wise are "making the most of the time, because the days are evil" (Eph. 5:16). Many commuters would translate *evil* as "tedious"; such are the hours on a train or in an automobile. So if one can redeem some of that time by thinking through a problem or dictating a memo, it may at least be a redeemed moment even if not a measurably sacred one.

While some have worked at commuting, others have learned to pray at it. Frank Laubach, a person so practical that he developed an epochal attack on illiteracy in his "each one teach one" program, was also the most prayerful of persons. He spent a great deal of time commuting to places where he would lecture or preach. He would choose a head some three, five, or six rows ahead of him on a train or plane and then concentrate on that unknown person, praying silently, until often that person—apparently feeling that someone was trying to get his or her attention—would turn around to look. Laubach, in spite of the tedium one can experience while traveling, found a way even in commuting to "feel God's pleasure."

In truth, we modern and postmodern people may have the best of all opportunities for prayer. Saintly folk in previous generations spoke of their "prayer closet," a place small enough and secluded enough that they could isolate themselves there to commune with God. For many commuters, the automobile could be the finest imaginable prayer closet. What is more private, more isolated than the steel and plastic interior of an automobile? Where better to speak confidentially to God, and where better to hear the voice of God in reply?

No doubt some fear that they would have little to say to God after speaking a few prayers for family and friends. But that's the point of the commuting scene; there are no other voices unless we invite them in by way of radio or some other device. In such isolation, the chances for communing with God are greatly improved. We might experience the kind of openness one sometimes has in an airplane conversation with a person we've never known and expect never to see again but with whom we become more candid than with a longtime associate or friend. Traveling does that to a person, and perhaps we can experience the same confiding in God.

I encourage what I call *spiritual isometrics*. Isometrics is a way of exercising by pitting one muscle against another, like putting a clenched fist in the palm of the other hand and pushing and resisting with full strength. Spiritual isometrics is the practice of pitting our prayerful thoughts against the circumstances of the day. This can be done in both positive and negative ways. That is, we can use the positive elements of the day for giving thanks: instead of ignoring or taking for granted the automobile's air-conditioning, the quality of the highway, the memory of a loyal friend, or the beauty of the countryside, we give thanks for them — thoughtfully, one by one, perhaps searching for adequate adjectives. Such searching will stretch the soul. If the situation is negative, we can offer prayers of petition: if the highway is under construction, pray for the workers; if the news of the morning is distressing, pray for those who are suffering. Don't fret, pray. Don't allow the circumstances of the day or culture to control your thoughts; rather, by prayer and thanksgiving transform the daily stuff of life into material for building the kingdom of God.

Saints develop a skill for seeing potential for the purposes of God wherever they are. It's a matter of heightened vision. We not only become more selective in what gets our attention but also we handle it more redemptively. We recognize that in our world there is that which is shoddy, or mediocre, or pain producing. But the heavenward soul sees the beauty as well, and the wonder of God's grace that can find springs of water in life's wilderness. And still more the heavenward mind comes increasingly to ask, "And what would you have me do about this pain, this ordinariness, this shadow of defeat?"

Many of us feel that it was probably easier to be a saint in a world that moved more slowly, where there was more quiet and less distraction, where solitude was easier to find. Let me suggest a counter thought: commuting may be the new frontier for the way of the saints. Where better to experience God than in an airplane or train coach, where on occasion you may, by careful listening, entertain an angel unawares? And where better to find solitude than in the privacy of an automobile? Where else can you be more alone? There is peculiar solitude on the airplane or the commuter train, where all those around you are either sleeping, reading, or occupying themselves with some electronic device. You can choose to entertain the Spirit of God.

Make such a place your prayer closet. Commune with God: in silence, or whispered prayer (spoken aloud if in your automobile), or in notes to your soul on a slip of paper. As the commute ends, as you gather your purse or computer bag, you may hear a voice in your soul: "Thank you, friend, for the pleasure of your company."

DAILY PROMISE

Today I will pray for some commuter, known or unknown, that whatever their journey, God will be their companion.

CHAPTER 6

WORKING

I grew up in what was known as the workingman's world. The definition of work was "the sweat of the brow." Numbers of people who were not even conventionally religious proudly described themselves with that biblical phrase without knowing its source. Some looked down on them for their menial labor and limited income, but when the working class were with their own kind, they spoke scornfully of those whose labor was less physical. "Never did an honest day's work in his life" was as severe a judgment as to call a person a thief or a whoremonger.

Nevertheless, many of the children of that world expected to get out of the life of sweat-labor, and to do so as quickly as possible. Many of my boyhood friends were first-generation Americans, and they had drunk the American dream to the full. They had their own vision of streets of gold; for them it came by hard work, but work that would deliver them from six-days-a-week, ten-hours-a-day labor. When our tenth-grade English teacher introduced us to Edwin Markham's poem "The Man with the Hoe" ("Who made him dead to rapture and despair . . .

Stolid and stunned, a brother to the ox?") we agreed in the school yard that God meant better for every human being and that we would throw ourselves into the battle to make it so. We'd begin by delivering ourselves from such labor.

Most, perhaps all, of my friends did just that. In the process, we changed our definition of labor. We learned that lecturing in a college classroom, writing for a newspaper or a radio network, or drawing up a legal brief was also labor. The brow sweat might be gone, but for some, the working hours were as long as for the parent who worked long hours six days a week. My question remains the same, however, whether one follows a plow, works in a factory, or composes music for a movie: Can one, does one, so work that he or she can say, "I feel God's pleasure"?

Enchanted as I was by the American dream, I spent many years feeling sorry for my father. He was born on a farm in northwest Iowa, but the wealth and success that some found eluded him. When several years of drought brought the farm to bankruptcy, my father and mother moved to the city, and my father took a job driving a delivery wagon powered by a team of horses. When the wagon became a truck, he became a truck driver, a deliveryman.

I was sure my father was better than that—that he could do something that paid better and was more prestigious. I was sorry that he spent his days carrying loads of dirty laundry from hotels, restaurants, and private homes, and returning the clean items in the afternoon or the following day. I knew the work because I worked with him on summer days or at busy times. I gloried in the muscular feeling but didn't find the work ennobling.

Many years later—as it happens, only a few months before my father died—we were reminiscing one evening. We began to talk about the laundries where he had worked and about some of the people who were employers or people at the ironing machines or the giant washtubs. "I was a lucky man," my father said. "I never knew a day when I dreaded going to work. Some people hated their jobs. I loved what I did." He was speaking the truth. I had never heard him complain about his work. Some customers were difficult, yes, and sometimes bosses seemed unfair, but I realized then that my father had never disliked his work; indeed, he loved it. He felt he was doing "honest labor." He was proud of the loyalty his customers showed to him when they were solicited by other laundries or cleaners. He enjoyed the hearty greetings in rundown hotels and modest eating places. He was known to his customers as John or Slim, and he knew them as Bill or Sally or Mike. When he said grace over our breakfast each morning, there was no resentment for the hours that lay ahead on the city streets or in the heat and steam of the laundry. He thought it was a wonderful thing to be an honest man with a job, with the knowledge that what he did helped other people and that his customers looked forward to seeing him.

My father might not have spelled it out theologically or philosophically, but his work brought pleasure to God. He didn't do it with Eric Liddell's Olympic grace, and not spectacularly *fast*, but he did it *well*. At Harvey's Laundry and at the Sunshine Laundry and Dry Cleaners, he did his work with grace. I don't know that he ever really envied anyone else's job. He would have been glad for a better salary, especially in the depth of the Great Depression, but he knew satisfaction in the work itself.

My father was an earnest Christian. He sang bass in the small church choir, often taught a boys' Sunday school class, and sometimes served on committees. If someone had asked him for his theology of work, my father would have answered in the simplest of terms: his work was honorable, he gave his employer his money's worth, and he tried in every way possible to take care of the needs of his customers, often to his disadvantage. Among his faithful customers were several houses of prostitution and of gambling. A scrupulous student might have told my father that he was assisting these people in their illegal and immoral businesses by handling their laundry and dry cleaning.

Somehow he saw them simply as human beings who were more to be pitied than censured.

Most of our world's work is still done by way of routine labor. Not everyone can start his or her own business, let alone survive in the vagaries of the economy. Few have the ability to be brain surgeons or the talent to write an opera or teach a course in philosophical ethics. So much of the world's work still involves some elements of drudgery, including some work that the world calls glamorous because it doesn't know the drudgery side. Some men to whom I was pastor and now are in the National Football League Hall of Fame let me know that they paid with multiplied hours of sweat and pain for the minutes they spent in the stadium spotlight on the weekend.

And some people—probably a majority—never get any kind of spotlight. They are hired and fired at the whims or the needs of others and often are paid not only meagerly but grudgingly. They rarely if ever hear a word of praise. And some of them, Lord have mercy, seem endowed with so few skills that it's hard to know what they bring to a job but good intentions and the need of a paycheck. In my mind, one of the saddest pictures in all of literature is in Charles William's *Descent into Hell* when an awkward worker is dismissed from his job. This was a routine experience for him—he was always the last one hired and the first one fired—but it's the kind of rejection one can never become finally accustomed to. This time, rather than returning home to tell his wife that he has again lost his job, he decides to take his own life.

Few go to that ultimate act, but who can estimate how many do a kind of vocational suicide, spending all their days in what is for them meaningless work? And what, too, shall we say for those who either misjudge their own abilities or never find the way to fulfill them? These are the people, so to speak, who know what a home run is but who spend their lives hitting singles or striking out. What shall we say for them? I sometimes think that the next best thing to saving souls is to save people from meaningless work or from becoming satisfied not to work. The God who works and who celebrates work's beauty by hallowing a seventh day to celebrate work surely understands the purpose-lostness of people who hate work, who do it without vision, or who never strive to do it really well.

Madeleine L'Engle wrote, "It is one of the sorrows of the Fall that work has become drudgery, rather than play. My actor husband and I were blessed that our work was also our play."[1] Some will say that it is easy to be excited about work when you're a renowned novelist or a Broadway actor. But then I think of my father, and of numbers of beautiful people I've known, who without putting it into words had a high theology of work. French Oliver, a Presbyterian evangelist and songwriter of the first half of the twentieth century, said it well in what sounds like a spiritual:

> There's a king and captain high,
> And He's coming by and by,
> And He'll find me hoeing cotton
> When He comes.
> And this God will be pleased.[2]

DAILY PROMISE

Today I will look for the wonder that is inherent
in the work I do. No task is ordinary to the
God who said, "Six days shalt thou labor."

CHAPTER 7

CLEANLINESS

My parents' generation almost surely knew the Bible better than today's generation does, but if you had asked one of them, "Where in the Bible is the verse 'Cleanliness is next to godliness'?" they would have answered, "I'm not sure exactly—probably Leviticus or Proverbs or one of Paul's letters. But it's there, I can tell you that." Their answer would have shown that their knowledge of the Bible wasn't perfect. It would also have demonstrated a good deal about their religion. It was everyday practical, and you demonstrated it as much by the way you kept your house and barn as by the way you sang a hymn.

Not only is this familiar proverb not in the Bible, but it's not very old—at least, not as wise sayings go or as our literary records reveal. The saying goes back to the latter part of the eighteenth century. It also has some established religious roots in that period. John Wesley, cofounder of the Methodist movement, said in one of his classic sermons, "Slovenliness is no part of religion." He continued that there was no text that condemned "neatness of apparel";

rather, that such was "a duty." Then he continued, "Cleanliness is, indeed, next to godliness."

If you know a little about the world of the eighteenth century in which Wesley lived and to which this proverb is credited, you know that slovenliness was more the pattern than cleanliness. It wasn't a world of running water; for the majority of the population, living in poverty or on poverty's borders, cleanliness was simply out of reach financially, or it was gotten at very great effort. But Wesley expected that his converts would change in all the basic particulars of their lives. Cleanliness was one of those particulars, and it wasn't easy to come by for large families crowded into settings of squalor.

The Hebrew Scriptures also came to birth in a world where cleanliness was gotten only by applied effort. The people of Israel lived in a land where water was scarce. Yet one of the key words in the Hebrew law was the adjective *clean*. It had to do more with holiness than with sanitation, but the two were closely related. A person afflicted with a disease thought to be contagious was said to be unclean. Certain foods were identified as unclean.

With it all, the laws of the Old Testament wove together sanitation and reverence—or if your prefer, godliness. They did so with candor. "You shall have a designated area outside the camp," their Law said. Take a trowel with you, the instruction continues, so that "when you relieve yourself outside, you shall dig a hole with it and then cover up your excrement." This is a law of cleanliness, but for the Israelites it was still more: "Because the Lord your God travels along with your camp, to save you and to hand over your enemies to you, therefore your camp must be holy, so that [God] may not see anything indecent among you and turn away from you" (Deut. 23:12–14).

Cleanliness was not simply next to godliness; it was an expression of godliness. This mood continued in the writings of the rabbinical scholars through the ages. Medieval rabbi Moses Maimonides wrote, "Physical cleanliness leads to the sanctification of the soul from reprehensible opinions."[1] That is, physical cleanliness has a kind of holy fallout, so that matters of the mind—"reprehensible opinions"—are cleansed along with soil from the body. So in the *Orchot Tzaddikim:* "Clothing, bed, table, especially dishes, indeed everything that we ever take in our hands, must be clean, sweet, pure; and above and beyond all, the body, made in the image of God."[2] In his *Instructions for Soldiers* (1777), George Washington wrote, "A soldier must admire the singular attention that was paid [in Israel] to the rules of cleanliness."[3] Thus, Washington employed the authority of Scripture to encourage cleanliness for men who were living in conditions where cleanliness was hard to maintain.

The close relationship of cleanliness to godliness may show itself in an unfortunate way—that is, in self-righteousness. Ralph Waldo Emerson felt that people who strove for cleanliness were inclined to have "a high mind about it," so that they looked down on those who were not so tidy. He had a point. A person with an orderly kitchen or living room or a well-organized garage can sound quite judgmental when discussing a neighbor whose own kitchen or living room or garage is dusty, disheveled, and deteriorating. And although such critics may not be particularly religious, their opinions of their untidy neighbors have definite moral overtones. This reminds us that one can be self-righteous without being religious. It reminds us, too, that some pursue cleanliness in a fashion that makes everyone else in their home or workplace uncomfortable.

Is there a virtue in cleanliness? And does cleanliness have any significant relationship to godliness? Particularly, is it possible that we might bring pleasure to God by our efforts toward cleanliness?

Our figures of speech reveal a great deal about our thinking. By this measure, cleanliness and orderliness rank high in our philosophy of life, and especially as taught in the Scriptures. When the psalmist asks, "Who shall ascend the hill of the Lord? / And who shall stand in his holy place?" he answers, "Those who have clean hands and pure hearts" (Ps. 24:3–4). The greatest of penitential prayers, Psalm 51, uses such language throughout: "Wash me thoroughly from my iniquity, / and cleanse me from my sin. . . . Purge me with hyssop, and I shall be clean; / wash me and I shall be whiter than snow." What the psalmist wants is "a clean heart," with a "new and right spirit" (Ps. 52:2, 7, 10).

We wouldn't expect the psalmist to rejoice in having soiled hands or to pray for a cluttered life. But that's the point. Something instinctive desires cleanliness and order, and when it is otherwise, we wonder what we can do about it. No wonder then that we use figures of speech from the clean and orderly to describe the goal of our spiritual lives.

But it isn't easy. Life itself isn't orderly, so dirt happens, plans go awry, things get out of place. The unwonted song of the tidy housekeeper is, "And just when I had everything so nice and orderly!"

The urge for cleanliness of surroundings and of person sometimes compels us with something like religious fervor. Two generations ago (I remember it well!), homemakers used terms that are now almost gone from our vocabulary: spring cleaning and fall cleaning. They were rituals. There were no set dates, such as Christmas or Independence Day; these tasks depended on more like a feeling in the air. Every homemaker knew it—some with foreboding and others with high anticipation. They might complain about it: the struggle for spotless windows, the dread of what they might find in some neglected corner, the sense that no one in the household would fully appreciate all that was being accomplished. But the excitement was palpable.

Sometimes there were rewarding surprises. With cleanliness came blessings: finding a misplaced item that everyone had given up for lost, the new beauty in a piece of furniture freshly polished, the sense of accomplishment in discarding what should have been thrown away the year before. The Bible tells of a time when a whole nation rejoiced in such a housecleaning. Good King Josiah commanded Judah's priests to repair the nation's temple, which had fallen into neglect. The process began with a general housecleaning. The workers discovered "the book of the law," the sacred document of God's dealings with their nation. The finding began a national spiritual renewal.

I can't promise such a discovery in a fall housecleaning or that long-postponed reorganization of closets, of your home or business office, of your garage, or of your filing cabinet. But I predict a high sense of satisfaction, that "Why didn't I do this long ago?" feeling. You will feel much more in control of your life. I remind myself, however, of the hazard in physical cleanliness: it's much easier to organize a filing cabinet or to clear the top of a desk than to clean the hidden corners of the soul. One dare not think that cleanliness is so close to godliness that a tidy appearance of body or auto is a reliable measure of the state of the soul.

Nevertheless, as John Wesley warned his new converts, slovenliness has no place in religion, and neatness of apparel is "a duty" for the Christian. This may be a rebuke to our generation, which glories in being "informal" even while wearing apparel that is relatively expensive. It's easy to become proud of that which may well deserve correction.

The Bible doesn't say that cleanliness is next to godliness, but it found cleanliness a worthy metaphor for holiness. As for orderliness, whatever else one finds in the creation story, it surely presents an orderly God. However long the days of creation may have been, God paused at intervals to announce, "That's *good*." Perhaps when we bring order to a desk, a garage, a kitchen, or a closet, or perhaps even when we take one last look in the mirror to check our wardrobe, God is pleased with what we're making of the things entrusted to our care.

DAILY PROMISE

Today I will see cleanliness and orderliness not as symbols of efficiency but as a God-honoring use of my time and ability.

CHAPTER 8

CONVERSATION

The ability to use words is one of the three or four greatest gifts possessed by the human race. Other creatures, ranging from the wonderfully organized ant colonies to the highly intelligent dolphins, have systems of communication, but nothing to compare with our human ability to invent and use words. The English language now has over a million words, most of them in technical and specialized fields, but all of them crucial to communication in the culture at large and to the thousands of subcultures in which we live.

Because words are so powerful, however, they are also a major hazard—perhaps the most dangerous in our possession. The Bible tells us that God created by way of speech—not by the skills of an engineer or an architect or a chemist, but with words. A cynic might well suggest that God created with words and that ever since, we humans have been in the process of dismantling the creation with the same instrument.

No wonder, then, that the Bible warns about the power of the tongue. The psalmist becomes a counselor: "Keep your tongue from evil, / and your lips from speaking deceit" (Ps. 34:13). The wisdom writer is emphatic: "With their mouths the godless / would destroy their neighbors" (Prov. 11:9). One reads that warning and thinks of many public personalities whose role in politics, business, or religion has been destroyed by the mouths of the godless. There are never enough retractions, never enough of setting the record straight to restore a reputation. There could be no stronger word and no truer one than this: "Death and life are in the power of the tongue, / and those who love it will eat its fruits" (Prov. 18:21).

James speaks in the same vigorous mood in the New Testament. Writing to early Christians, the apostle described the tongue as an ultimate measure of spiritual integrity. People who think themselves religious but who do not "bridle their tongues" are deceiving themselves; "their religion is worthless" (Jas. 1:26). If you've been part of a conversation that moved rather easily from pious speech to destructive gossip (as most of us have), you wonder how we find a segue that leads so easily from the one to the other. We want James to tell us that the power of Christ will break the power of the tongue, but the apostle seems almost to concede that the situation is hopeless: we humans have learned how to bring every species of animals and reptiles under our control, "but no one can tame the tongue—a restless evil, full of deadly poison" (Jas. 3:7).

Jesus spoke an even more alarming word. "I tell you," he said, "on the day of judgment you will have to give an account for every careless word you utter; for by your words you will be justified, and by your words you will be condemned" (Matt. 12:36). Our Lord spoke similar powerful judgments regarding our care of the sick, the poor, the imprisoned, the helpless (Matt. 25:41–46). That judgment seems to offer more hope than Jesus' warning about careless words, because ministering to those in need is an act within reach, if we care so to dedicate ourselves, but words seem so spontaneous as to be almost involuntary and thus out of our control.

It's enough to make one pledge oneself to a monastic order of silence. But that won't work. As surely as the tongue can bring hell on the daily scene, so too can it bring heaven. Words can destroy reputations, but they can also protect and enhance them. Words can break the heart, but they can heal it even more dramatically. Words are a powerful trust from God, perhaps the most decisive power entrusted to us humans. We aren't allowed, therefore, to seek some neutral island where we stop talking. We must learn to employ this most powerful instrument so that we use it with divine health, love, and joy.

That brings us to the matter of conversation, including its written forms: the letter, email, text message, and all forms of social media. Even in this age of texting, though, spoken conversation is the largest user of words. It is also the most difficult to control, since it is an active form. Any written communication has at least some fraction of time for thought, but oral communication as generally practiced doesn't encourage periods of reflection.

I love conversation, but I avoid talkers. Talkers are so excited about their own stories and opinions that they don't listen well. Often they hear incorrectly because they hear for the purpose of reply rather than of understanding. Their personal punctuation is the comma or the semicolon, because they want to avoid a conclusion. When the other person speaks, they're devoted to listening only for the period, the question mark, or the exclamation point, which signals that they can speak again. *Conversation* is identified by that prefix, *con*, which means "together with," as in a mutual give and take. We can pay another person no greater compliment than to listen to them carefully.

Lord (Thomas) Macaulay was a brilliant English politician, historian, and essayist; you'll find scores of his sayings in collections of quotations. Yet there's something significant in Lady Holland's memoirs when she quotes,

"He has occasional flashes of silence that make his conversation perfectly delightful"[1] Probably more such "flashes of silence" would have enhanced his conversation still more. Someone might remind me that the books of quotations don't record any of Macaulay's silences. True. But remember this: In conversation, it isn't a matter of how many words we speak, but of how many words the other person hears. If the other person has turned us off, for good reason or bad, we've stopped speaking, whether we know it or not. Conversation has two parts: speaking and hearing. And true conversation depends as much on good hearing as on good speaking.

Many of us have discovered that in some company we speak much more eloquently than in others. Other persons can bring out the best in us. It can be a high compliment for someone to say, "You're a good listener," if this means that by your listening you have unloosed the ability of the other person to speak clearly and thoughtfully. And that's half, and sometimes more, of the making of a good conversation.

Good conversation also challenges the character. I've been privileged to be in some conversations where I left wanting to be a better person. And it was rarely, if ever, a conversation in which the other person "preached" to me. Rather, what made the difference was the character of the other person and the goodness he or she conveyed both in listening and in speaking.

I love (I'm using the word intentionally) good conversation. I enjoy the person with a sense of humor and also with a capacity for pathos. I respond to the well-turned phrase—not the memorized one, but the one that springs naturally from the context of ideas and of friendship. I find stimulation in persons who can put ideas in a different setting, revealing insights I hadn't seen before. I am blessed by those whose empathy makes any discussion of persons an occasion of grace.

I'm not sure how long a good conversation can last. I've known some that extended for hours, with depth and value all the way. Nevertheless, I often ponder the opinion of John Wesley, that expert in the use of time. He lived by the rule "Few can converse profitably above an hour."[2] I've known many conversations that would have been more worthwhile and better remembered if they had come to an end an hour earlier.

Jesus left his followers with a remarkable promise: "For where two or three are gathered in my name, I am there among them" (Matt. 19:20). The number is significant. That is, it seems to refer to a more intimate, personal gathering than a larger, public occasion of worship. We should give more attention to the value of daily Christian friendship, knowing God is present in these interactions as much or more than in large corporate worship. What if, more often, two or three believers—family, friends, acquaintances, whatever their level of faith—would think of their conversations as an engagement of faith? Not simply by assigned subject matter, but by the quality of caring, hearing, and speaking. Might we more often sense that Christ has joined the conversation? That there are not two present, but three; not three, but four; not a foursome in the restaurant booth, but five? Might it be that our conversation would thus give pleasure to God?

I'm altogether sure of it.

DAILY PROMISE

Today I will look for an opportunity to listen well
and to speak judiciously. Every word reflects
on the God who created by way of words.

CHAPTER 9

GIVING AND
RECEIVING

It's impossible to separate giving and receiving. There can't be a giver unless there's also a receiver, and you can't receive unless somebody, for whatever reason, decides to give. Givers might feel superior to receivers, especially if the receiver needs what the giver has. But when people have no one to whom to give, they lose some of their basic humanness. We need to be needed. "Is it wrong, Pastor, for me to ask God to let me die?" the elderly infirm sometimes ask me. "No one needs me anymore, so there's really no reason for me to go on living." Translated, they are saying, "I need somebody to give to."

As I note at other times in this book, we humans are caught in an interlocking mystery of human relationships. Whether we like it or not, we need others, and others need us.

But it's not simple. Someone has said that if he saw someone coming who intended to do him good, he would run as quickly as possible in the opposite direction. It's difficult to receive because to receive indicates that in some way we're in need. That's a confession we don't like to make. Often the person who gives must be a bit of a diplomat, else the gift becomes an offense. A generous, well-meaning person can easily irritate when intending to bless.

This is especially true in American culture. For generations, our culture has bred us for self-sufficiency: make our own opportunities, fight our own battles, pay our own way. When I hear persons use the word *socialism* derisively, I know that what they especially resent is the idea that they—or anybody else—should be dependent on anyone but themselves. We like the feeling that we've earned what we have. I enjoy the stories of those who have worked their way upward, but I see that sometimes their experience makes them forget the help they've received along the way. All of us are receivers, and all of us should be givers.

I remember when I learned to be a giver. My parents taught me some basics, but it was my sixth-grade Sunday school teacher, who taught me to tithe my income (which was very meager at the time) and to expect to give beyond that. It was a thrilling experience. Giving blesses a person with a great sense of goodwill and even of power. It was harder to learn how to be a receiver. My parents made a good start. They gave to me and taught me to say "Thank you" and even to understand that I had reasons to be grateful. One family was especially sensitive in recognizing the nature of my needs; it was easy to thank them. But we were poor, especially as the Great Depression hit our household, and our neediness grated on me.

One can't be a good receiver without a rather well developed sense of humility. Perhaps some escape the problem with the attitude "I've got it coming to me," but that attitude violates the giver-receiver relationship. If I think I deserve what is given to me, the giver ceases to be a giver and becomes a payer. By contrast, givers can feel that receivers are altogether deserving and perhaps that life itself owes those persons more, so they give with the sense of paying some sort of debt, real or intangible.

It is nearly impossible to give to some people because their tastes are so exclusive that someone else's gift rarely is right. Often such persons are themselves especially sensitive givers; they spend much time finding just the right gift, then packaging and delivering it in the most appealing way. But their very excellence in giving makes them poor receivers.

In a perfect world, the givers and receivers would know exactly how to use their respective powers. They would know that they were needed and would not think better of themselves for fulfilling their need. Those who are rich in money, power, and influence can do so much for those who lack these benefits, but their very power makes them poor in unprejudiced friendship. Moses could stare down Pharaoh, but he needed the priceless counsel of his father-in-law, Jethro. With all of his power and personality, King David was in danger without the clear-eyed loyalty of the prophet Nathan and the general Joab. Elijah apparently feared no one and seemed to enjoy his lone-wolf status, but he needed young Elisha to feed his lonely soul.

If someone doesn't know how to give, that person's wealth becomes a curse. Jesus said simply and directly that it is difficult for the rich to enter the kingdom of heaven. Of course! Being rich, they find it difficult if not impossible to empathize with those who are poor. If whatever you want has always been available to you, how can you understand those who simply haven't enough to survive? One blinded by wealth needs nothing short of a divine revelation to see clearly how desperate is poverty and how powerful (and therefore, self-condemning) is abundance. The poor need wisdom to use what they get. The rich need both wisdom and grace to realize how much they have and to realize the obligation they have to share intelligently and graciously with others.

Of course, poverty and wealth, and giving and receiving, are not limited to physical possessions and monetary wealth. The gifted musician must give knowledge to the novice who hopes someday to become a maestro. The writer who has learned how to shape words into beauty must give time to the student who doesn't know the difference between the graceful word and the ungainly one. I still marvel that Mari Sandoz not only encouraged me in a summer writing seminar a lifetime ago but also bothered a year or two later to drop me a note to ask how my writing was progressing. She gladly gave; I was exhilarated to receive.

Ultimately, the biggest thing any of us can give another is time. Time is a piece of our very self. It is, as we so often say and need continually to realize, our only irreplaceable resource. Here is a place where the rich and the poor stand on level ground, or nearly so. I can be a giver if I am the server in the restaurant and listen carefully enough to answer your inquiry helpfully, and I can be a giver if I am the one being served and I give you my kind attention when you ask, "Are you enjoying your meal?" Of course, it helps if I give a generous tip! I can give my time in someone's hour of loneliness—including that person whose loneliness seems inexhaustible—and in the birthday remembered, the note or email written, the prayer offered, the call made.

Sometimes as one reads the Old Testament, God seems unduly anxious for attention. When the prophet excoriates the people for forgetting God and says that God is unhappy about this, God seems very un-Godlike. Perhaps, however, this is only to remind us not only that God is the ultimately Giver but also that God chooses to be the needy Receiver. Here is something of the profound humility of God: God the Giver is also God the would-be Receiver. If God had isolated the divine Self from our human race, there would be no giving and therefore no need of receiving. Naturally, we like to perceive God as the Giver, especially since we are so often suppliants. But giving and receiving are inseparable. God, in humility, accepts the role of Receiver, and in a fashion that sometimes seems almost petulant, asks how we could forget to give the one thing we have: our love and adoration.

It's easy to see that God is a Giver. The abundance of creation and its infinite variety portray a God who delights in giving. Beyond all of that and quite beyond our comprehension, God gives us salvation via his Son, Jesus Christ. God is our lesson in giving: to see what the other person needs, to recognize the particular dimensions of that need, and then to give it.

But God is also a Receiver. The Bible reveals a God who welcomes our love, our thanks, and our worship. God surely has enough, yet God chooses to need what we humans can give and receives our gifts with pleasure. God is our lesson in receiving: to have the humility to need what others can give and to know the difference. Thus, the most moving of prayers, Psalm 51, notes that God might not be pleased with our burnt offerings but rejoices in "a broken and contrite heart" (Ps. 51:15). This reminds us that the spirit of the giver is crucial to the quality of the gift.

Giving and receiving are both extraordinary human enterprises. Some of us are better at one than the other, but perhaps it's rare for a person to be truly good at both. To do both really well is godly. When it happens, God is surely and deeply pleased.

DAILY PROMISE

Today I will give someone some of my time, the essence of who I am, and I will humble myself to receive sensitive gratitude.

CHAPTER 10

LAUGHING AND CRYING

Recently a cherished friend forwarded to me an item from a British newspaper. It was insightful, poignant, and funny. I emailed my thanks with a question: "Am I supposed to laugh or to cry?" He replied, as I expected, "Both."

Two generations ago, traveling theater companies that worked America's small towns had a phrase to describe the melodramas that were their forte: "a play that makes the dimples catch the tears." That concept has been at the heart of the best tales since the first time several people gathered around an elder and said, "Tell us a story." Laughing and crying may seem to be opposites. In truth, they are first cousins. No wonder ancient dramatists carried two masks, laughter and tears, to be lifted at proper intervals throughout their performance. It's in that spirit that I link them together for our purposes.

We see the two together at weddings and funerals. Weddings are events of separating and joining. You can't have one without the other, and separating generally means tears, and joining means laughter. Consider funerals. Except for those of unmitigated tragedy, there are always moments of laughter at such services, evoked by some anecdote that reminds mourners of why they loved the deceased, and the laughter gives greater substance to the tears. When the ancient wise man tells us that "for everything there is a season," of course he includes "a time to weep, and a time to laugh"—and then, as if to underline his point, he continues, "a time to mourn, and a time to dance" (Eccl. 3:1, 4). But he doesn't tell us that sometimes the two come so closely linked that we're not sure which belongs at our right hand at the table of the soul's hospitality.

The deeper and more fulfilling the laughter, the more painful the tears. A child is born, and the tears of childbirth are swallowed up in the rejoicing of the birth. The parents agree that they've never known joy to compare with this hour. Only an oafish, heartless friend would interrupt their joy to tell them that this baby will also (innumerable times) give them tears such as they might never otherwise know. The more heartfelt the laughter, the more wrenching the tears. A cynic might warn, "Don't laugh too much, because you will cry proportionately," and the cynic would be right. Nevertheless, those of us who have known such combinations of laughing and crying will testify almost unanimously that the laughter is worth the tears and that nothing can really take the laughter from us. Whatever, laughing and crying are the closest of kin, so we shouldn't be surprised that they come to life's festivals together.

The first specific reference to laughter in the Bible is not the laughter of joy but of incredulity, first from Abraham and then from Sarah (Gen. 17:17; 18:12). When God assured each of them that they would have a child in their old age, they both thought it a bit of a joke, so they laughed. When that unlikely child was born, Abraham named him *Laughter* (Isaac), and Sarah fully enjoyed the joke: "God has brought laughter for me; everyone who hears will laugh with me" (Gen. 21:6). Some years later their laughter came to a place of profound tears, surely, when Abraham faced the test of the sacrificing of Isaac (Gen. 22:1–14). It seems clear that Abraham was confident his son would survive; nevertheless, he could hold to that confidence only by a supreme test of faith, and that test must have been at a place of tears. The writer of Genesis tells us nothing about Sarah's involvement in this gothic event, so we have no way of measuring the sorrow she might have felt. But it was there, no doubt about that.

Early in the book of Genesis there are pictures of God's laughter and tears. The words are not used, but the moods are there and are unmistakable. The quality of laughter runs steadily through the creation story, as the course of events is marked by the announcement that God "saw that it was good" and then, at completion of the immediate project, that it "was very good." I hear laughter in that report — or at the least, a cosmic smile. But a few generations later, the human story had deteriorated to such a degree that "the Lord was sorry that he had made humankind on the earth, and it grieved him to his heart" (Gen. 6:6). At that point, we observe divine tears; God is weeping. You cannot love enough to laugh without raising the possibility of sorrow to the point of crying — not even if you are God.

Perhaps this is when we are closest to God, in the moments of laughing and crying. Perhaps that's why every good prayer includes both "Thank you" and "I'm sorry," because life is both smiles and tears.

And what is true of divine communication, via prayer, is true also of good human communication. So the apostle Paul commanded, "Rejoice with those who rejoice, weep with those who weep" (Rom. 12:15). Paul taught this truth because he knew that it can be difficult to enter into either experience. Awkwardness and a sense of inadequacy keep us from weeping with those who weep. We wonder what to say, never fully convinced that long speeches or profound counsel are rarely needed at times of weeping. Our modern and postmodern culture finds it especially difficult to enter into another person's pain. But the more that suffering is institutionalized and professionalized, the more we need people who will give it a personal face.

Rejoicing often presents a different problem. When you're on the losing team, it's difficult to rejoice with the winner. When your neighbor's child wins the scholarship, it isn't natural to offer congratulations while your own son or daughter is huddled in a corner of disappointment. When you wonder how long you can keep your job, how do you rejoice with a colleague who has just received a promotion with grand benefits? Paul was recommending a high level of Christian love, indeed.

With it all, we need to remind ourselves that neither laughing nor crying is necessarily good. We remember the iconic picture of Adolf Hitler dancing in glee at the report of a military victory. There is a whole category of laughter under the heading *derisive*. Some laughter comes from humor that belittles someone else's ethnic, social, intellectual, or economic identity. Laughter can be profoundly cruel.

This is true, too, with our tears. Tears are necessary and important. We need them as an outlet for feelings that can otherwise be driven inside, where they eat away at the soul. We need them to relieve the pain of someone else's loneliness or grief. But tears can also become an emotional addiction; we call it *self-pity*. We can spend tears so lavishly on ourselves that there are few left for anyone else. Apparently there is no human virtue that cannot be misshapen into a vice.

So what shall we do with these lovely twins, laughing and crying? How can our exercise of laughter and tears bring pleasure to God?

As a starter, we need more of both—more of the real thing, that is. As surely as nature abhors a vacuum, so do our souls. We humans are emotional creatures. The expression of these emotions varies with ethnic and cultural groups, but they belong to all of us, the poker-faced as well as the teary-eyed. But our culture has become so accomplished at producing synthetic varieties of emotions that many have no idea how to experience or cope with the real thing—that is, how to experience true laughter or to cope with real tears. We are, increasingly, a drug culture and have now added legal marijuana to our stock. I feel very sorry for those who don't know how to laugh unless they're a little "high." The culture has made it so. And I'm sorry for us, that so often we turn too soon to pills that prevent nature from doing its natural healing, via sleep and some tears. We would do well to learn how to laugh without artificial stimulation, and to cry without guilt or apology.

Laughing and crying are holy gifts. God made us with equipment that is essentially singular to us humans. Thank God that you can laugh and then ask God to quicken and sharpen your sense of humor. And thank God that you can cry, for yourself and for others, as well. Be a little sorry for yourself occasionally—it's not fatal if taken in small portions—and spend lots of it on those who need someone else to cry for them.

Then look to the God who equipped you so generously with these gifts of laughter and tears. Some religions and ancient philosophies teach that whatever god there may be is impassive and impassable, a creature that cannot be moved by pain or joy. The Bible, however, shows us a God who experiences joy and brokenness. Therefore, as you look toward God, give thanks. Give it through your laughter and tears. As you do, you will give pleasure to the God who made you so that you can both laugh and cry.

DAILY PROMISE

Today I will be ready to join someone in laughter and to share in someone's tears.

CHAPTER 11

⁓⁓

RELATIONSHIPS

The most tightly packed cemetery in America is on Hart Island, in New York's Long Island Sound. It is often referred to as a burial place for the nameless dead. While it is true that many of the persons buried there are nameless, a more accurate description would be the *unclaimed* dead. New York has more than its share of such persons, not simply because it is a very large city but because it is a place where so many choose to lose themselves when they're fleeing from the past or when they feel that families and friends want nothing to do with them. Hart Island's potter's field is a place for persons without relationships.

Prison inmates from Riker's Island perform the burials. Several years ago a newspaper writer visited with the men who prepare the graves week after week. One of them said, "One thing I've learned from Hart Island is that I don't want to die a nobody, with nothing or no one to care about me. . . . I guess it's the loneliest place in the world, and I pray, and will always pray, for the lonely and lost souls of Hart Island."[1]

Hart Island is a good place to contemplate the way our human personalities interlock. As the book of Genesis opens, God smiles repeatedly on the unfolding creation and says that it is *good*. But then, in a reprise of a portion of the story, God looks at the human creature and says that something is *not good*: "It is not good that the man should be alone" (Gen. 2:18). No matter all the beauty of nature, the presence of other living creatures—birds, animals, fish, insects—and even, indeed, a sense of the presence of God are still not enough. We humans need one another. We're made that way.

I'm not speaking about love or even about friendships. I'm using a broader word: *relationships*. Those connections with neighbors, colleagues, acquaintances, even strangers—people we interact with on some level. Both friendship and love involve some degree of emotion, which is not necessarily true of relationships. Relationships are both less and more than friendship. Less in that they don't necessarily claim an intimate place in our lives, and more in that because of their number they often make a larger total claim on our time than do friendships or loves. Obviously, every friendship or bond of love is a relationship, but every relationship is not necessarily an experience of love or friendship.

We have numbers of relationships every day. They come to us by letter, email, text, telephone, Skype, or face-to-face encounter. Many of these relationships are unintentional yet sometimes peculiarly intimate. Standing in a crowded public transportation space or at an entertainment or sporting event, we touch bodies with people we don't know and will never see again. So too with verbal communication; some of it is not only without intention, but forced upon us. For instance, when in a public place someone engages too loudly in a cell phone conversation, we learn more about this person, her business, or her family life than we want to know. We don't desire this relationship, and the person surely doesn't intend for us to be taken into her confidence, though one might judge otherwise by the volume of the conversation. Sometimes the relationship goes a step deeper than expected; overhearing about someone's surgery, job loss, broken friendship, or troubled marriage, we feel their pain to the point where we choose to pray for them. Henry Wadsworth Longfellow spoke of relationships as "ships that pass in the night"; in our day, they are voices that surround us in the airport waiting area or from a nearby table at a restaurant. "Only a look and a voice," Longfellow said, "then darkness again and a silence."[2]

Relationships are mysterious and unpredictable. Some seem of no likely consequence, yet when that delivery person transfers to another company or the server in the restaurant moves on, we feel a peculiar loneliness. John Donne said so memorably, "Any man's death diminishes me, because I am involved in Mankind."[3] I want to say in the same fashion that any person's life makes me a larger person. I can't say that I enjoy every person I meet, nor can I honestly say that I would anticipate a continuing relationship with each one. But they're human, as I am. We share the same heritage of earth's sod and God's breath, and an overwhelmingly similar set of genes. We belong to one another, like it or not, so it would be good for us to appreciate one another's worth and the wonder of our relationships.

These relationships come in infinite variety. They can be as brief as a mall encounter or as incidental as the person who rides the same commuting train or bus five days a week. They can be as physically close as the person who sat next to us in a college lecture course yet whose name never got a permanent place in our memory. They can be invisible—the person offering customer service by phone or online chat, for example. None of these relationships is lasting, yet each one has its place in one's life. They are pieces of the jigsaw puzzle of daily living.

Sometimes the brief, incidental relationship is memorable. Those of us who travel a good deal have learned that only occasionally does the person in the next seat go beyond a perfunctory greeting; some, not even that. But I've had memorable conversations with persons I've never seen since and whose names I don't know. I'm altogether certain that some people have had an incidental travel visit that ended not only in friendship but in love and marriage. I don't know of such, mind you, but the odds are better than the lottery. Last week, a substantial number of people in a small city just down the road from where I live bought a tombstone for a street person in their town. Few knew his name, but hundreds knew him by sight or by frequent, passing greeting. When they learned he had died, they felt the loss, and when they heard there was no real marker for his burial place, they saw to one. Relationships! Who can judge their importance? Who can say what place they have in eternity?

In a sense, the first generation of Christians was vulnerable in the world of relationships. They were a minority group that existed at the possible whim of governments and of other religious and secular bodies. Now and again, with little obvious provocation, they could become the objects of arrest, of prosecution and persecution, and of mob violence. Under such circumstances, they could justifiably be wary of every stranger. Who could say what malice that unknown person might have in mind?

Yet in such a world the person writing the letter to the Hebrews told his people, "Do not neglect to show hospitality to strangers, for by doing that some have entertained angels without knowing it" (Heb. 13:2). Perhaps the writer was referring to the story of Abraham, when he entertained the visitors who were headed to Sodom and Gomorrah, but the language seems to suggest more immediate reports. Whatever the basis for this counsel, I marvel at the readiness to offer a relationship: "Stay in our home for the night." "You have no place to eat? By all means, have your evening meal with us." Believers were sure that in extending kindness to a stranger, they pleased God and fulfilled the teachings of their faith. If that be so, then why not also expect that a miracle (an angelic visitor!) might come their way?

I am not privy to the ways of angels, and in a world where, on any given day, one's email inbox can include an appeal from some unknown name in a foreign country who needs just $1,590 to replace a lost briefcase and some traveler's checks, I'm cautious. How do we read the New Testament writer's call for hospitality? What do we do with relationships in a steadily more secular culture? Each instance should be seen in its own setting, but for a general theology of relationships I cast my vote with C. S. Lewis. In his memorable sermon-essay "The Weight of Glory," he insists, "There are no *ordinary* people. You have never talked to a mere mortal." And because this is so, while our relationships are by no means all solemn, there should be in them "no flippancy, no superiority, no presumption." Lewis concludes with a daring statement: "Next to the Blessed Sacrament itself, your neighbour is the holiest object presented to your senses."[4]

It seems to me that Jesus made the same point in another way when he said that on the day of judgment we will be evaluated by the way we have treated the sick, the homeless, the imprisoned, the hungry—nearly all of them relationships of a quite impersonal kind—yet persons who are Jesus in disguise.

In even the most "ordinary" relationship there's the possibility that we will give pleasure to God. God's creation and incarnation tell us that all persons matter; therefore, every relationship is rich with eternal potential.

DAILY PROMISE

Today I will look for the unique depth
that is part of even the most occasional
and transitory of relationships.

CHAPTER 12

PLAYING

Anthropologists, theologians, and poets have all speculated about the antiquity of play, but it's hard to find anything substantial to support those speculations. So many things that we now do for recreation were originally matters of survival. Today many play at hunting and fishing, but our ancestors saw success at these activities as a matter of life and death. We make a sport of running, throwing javelins, and wrestling; long ago, the race was a deadly contest with a wild animal, the javelin was a war instrument, and wrestling was the showdown hour when you caught your enemy or the enemy caught you. One wonders if the excitement of today's play is somehow buried in our primitive memory with the peculiar excitement of survival. Perhaps when fans say that they "live and die" with their teams, their figure of speech has deeper roots than they realize.

The Bible says little about sports as such until the apostle Paul refers to wrestling, boxing, and racing as metaphors for elements of the spiritual life; in doing so, Paul reflects the Grecian world of the Olympics, which were a significant part of life and entertainment in the first century.

Earlier, the psalmist spoke of God blessing him so that he could "leap over a wall" (Ps. 18:29), but the reference is in the setting of battle. Physical prowess was praised in a variety of ways, especially running, but in the efficiency of work or battle rather than in the field of play.

Almost surely, children over the centuries have played, especially in the manner that is still a favorite: by imitating grown-ups. But it seems clear that play was not commonplace in the kind of adult world where many lived by subsistence agriculture or the precarious availability of wild food, nor in the early periods of the Industrial Revolution, when children were drafted into the workforce. The secret was to keep alive, and those whose resources left time for play were relatively few.

But times have changed, and they continue to do so even more dramatically. Well over a century ago, in a world much less made for play than ours, Robert Louis Stevenson wrote, "The world is so full of a number of things, / I'm sure we should all be as happy as kings."[1] If life is to be valued by its opportunities for play, the kings of previous centuries look like paupers compared to millions of people today—many of whom, unfortunately, struggle with boredom even as they seek new venues of play.

Our ancestors looked for opportunities to play, and our contemporary culture is sure that there are yet more undiscovered fields of play that will bring more pleasure than our ancestors ever knew or than we knew last year. And since one of the elements of play is doing that which is different, certainly no generation has had such vistas of possibility as ours. Our human inclination to envision a larger tomorrow is grand, and it predicts that our children and grandchildren will enjoy toys, games, distractions, marvels, and experiences beyond today's most advanced—or, God forbid, most debased—thinking.

What is play? And what is its purpose? Perhaps the best one-word definition of *play* is "diversion." This also describes its purpose. To play is to escape the ordinary.

Eating out is play for the person who prepares the family meals every day, every week. But for those whose daily routine includes a Danish and coffee en route to work, followed by a business luncheon or a bowl of soup at the desk, and ending at a restaurant for dinner with a spouse or friend, play is concocting and preparing a meal at home for guests. Play is diversion from the ordinary, unless the ordinary itself is extraordinarily fulfilling.

For many—perhaps far more than we know—drugs are a major factor of play. Drugs provide an escape from the ordinary, a diversion. They offer a flight from boredom: the boredom of work, of persons, of problems, or of life itself. Those who speak of a drug as providing a *high* are telling us that for them too much of life is a *low*. In time, of course, the chemical high becomes increasingly necessary. It also becomes more demanding, because life's lows become more than ever something to flee from.

Drugs require few if any skills. Most forms of play—whether dancing, team sports, golf, or table games—move from rudimentary to sophisticated skills; that is not so with drugs. Nor do drugs require other persons; others may or may not contribute to the experience. The drug itself is the diversion, with no help needed. Those whose play quickens the mind, activates the body, or stimulates the social impulses might resent my referring to drugs as a kind of play. But play is like almost all of life's activities in that it can be exalting, mundane, or debasing. Drugs are the most tragic face of play, because they are the most deceiving and most destructive. Thus we speak of drugs not as a diversion but as an addiction. Mind you, probably any form of play can become addictive, whether chess, horseshoes, or ballroom dancing, but the power of drugs is more frightening because of the chemical component.

Play is for those who can afford it—enough money, yes, but more especially, time. When people lived a subsistence existence, they had little or no time for play. I wonder if some tribal peoples even had time enough to realize that play existed. They may have needed diversion, but there was no time to seek it. Some would also say, though perhaps cautiously, that play is for those who need it. For those persons whose lives are full and fulfilled by work, family, or the sheer wonder of living, there is little or no need for diversion; the matters that fill their time are so satisfying that diversion is itself an intrusion.

So what shall we say for play? If it is only an escape from boredom, we might argue that life should be changed at its core, so that the need for diversion is not so insistent. But if the old saying (dating back nearly four hundred years) is right in warning that "all work and no play makes Jack a dull boy," then play is necessary to normal, healthy living, and if we don't allow it a place in life, we are poorer for it. Play may be to the rest of life what inhaling is to exhaling, except that it is not so insistent or so organized.

Is play, perhaps, a version of the Sabbath? That is, is play—as diversion—a form of rest? Is it a gift from God, a seventh of life that equips us for better use of the six other parts? Should the Sabbath itself be the highest form of play, by which worship, rest, family, friendship, and intentional goodness add a lilt to that which is otherwise routine? G. K. Chesterton, in his own way the most devout of persons, was more emphatic: "The true object of all human life is play. Earth is a task garden; heaven is a playground."[2]

Chesterton enjoyed saying things that shocked people, but he was usually making a serious point in doing so. In what way might heaven be a playground? That is, is play holy in itself? Do we make life more serious than it ought to be so that in the process we sour even the happy moments? I marvel (sadly) at those persons who, being greeted on the beauty of a perfectly lovely day, quickly answer, "We'll pay for it next week," or, "The almanac says it's going to be one of the worst winters." I also marvel at those parents who have organized their children's baseball, soccer, or basketball games into the serious business of leagues and tournaments and championships. When I visit the neighborhoods of my childhood, I pause behind a not-very-nice downtown building where I frequently spent summer afternoons throwing a tennis ball against a wall and playing out a game in my imagination. There were no children my age in the area, so I became my own competition. I won trophies that no one ever saw.

Perhaps we should ask some serious questions about play. Can it be an end in itself, or do we feel we must justify it by showing what gain it has brought to us? That is, is it okay for play simply to be an end in itself? And if one is pure in heart, can play truly be a kind of Sabbath in its own right? Recall that Eric Liddell became a champion, but his fulfillment wasn't in the victories; he loved to run, and when he ran, he felt God's pleasure.

Does God find pleasure in the colt that frisks in excited awkwardness in the field or the goose that glides so gracefully into the lake? Or does God smile when a preschooler giggles at something a busy adult doesn't see, or when an eleven-year-old lies in the summer grass and dreams of she knows not what?

I think so. I can't prove it, but I think so. I cast my vote for healthy play. With Chesterton, I think it has something to do with heaven.

DAILY PROMISE

Today I will look for the heavenly quality in
my play and will settle for nothing less.

CHAPTER 13

LOVING

Of all the daily activities through which we humans might give pleasure to God, surely none is more in line with the nature of God than loving. The Bible tells us that "God is love" and that "love is from God" (1 John 4:7–8). We humans are blessed with a capacity for love; therefore, we can hardly go wrong in pleasing God when we pursue love.

Well, not necessarily.

As a pastor, I heard hundreds—perhaps thousands—of stories of human love, and I estimate that they were divided rather equally between regret and rejoicing. I expect that the poetry, drama, and novels about love divide at the same percentage. Indeed, with novelists and poets being who they are, there are probably more love poems and stories of unrequited or misplaced love than of fulfilled love. The classic fairy tale tells of a princess who kissed a frog that then was transformed into a handsome prince. In real life there may be more cases of kissed frogs that remain frogs, sometimes bringing the princess herself down to frog level. This love business is highly precarious, particularly when we invest in it the way most love investors do—with all they have! But of course, isn't that essentially the definition of love, that we give it all we've got?

We've made matters still more complicated by the way we use the word *love*. Long before we had taken all meaning from the word *awesome* by careless usage, we did full violence to the word *love*. Our bumper stickers announce that we love Texas, the Yankees, our poodle, or our country. I overhear conversations where love for grandchildren and fettuccini are announced within the same minute with the same verb and rather comparable vigor.

There's no question but that we need synonyms for love as both noun and verb or, at the least, more care in our use of these power-packed words. Still, it isn't surprising that our definition of love is so vague. This is a long-standing human problem. When Eve took a long look at the forbidden fruit, she saw that it would be good to eat, that it was a delight to the eyes, and that it would be nourishing beyond anything else she had thus far experienced. I'm sure that when she offered the fruit to Adam it was with the recommendation, "Try this. You'll just *love* it." There is almost always some element of attractiveness in that which we love, whether the object is fruit, pet, spouse, child, art, or virtue. We "fall in love" with all manner of things.

But we're stuck with this word. Jesus put an eternal imprimatur on it. When an inquirer asked him what was the first commandment—that is, what commandment summarized and included all the rest—he answered, "'You shall love the Lord your God with all your heart, and with all your soul, and with all your mind.' This is the greatest and first commandment. And a second is like it: 'You shall love your neighbor as yourself'" (Matt. 22:37–39). It's difficult, indeed impossible, to get away from that word *love*.

The point is this: Love, of itself, is not necessarily good. Love is shaped by many forces—heredity, upbringing, experience, learning, and acquired taste, to name some of the more obvious ones. We can love wisely or foolishly. And sometimes the otherwise-wisest people are the most foolish when it comes to love. In matters of romance, people sometimes speak of young love as *puppy love*. It's an apt term, but it's not that different from one that we don't often use: *tired-old-dog love*. We don't always get wiser with age, because our wisdom doesn't keep up with our changing perception. That is, our experience tends to be a step ahead of our wisdom; that's how it is that we learn from experience.

Nonetheless, love is a God-ordained and God-blessed instinct, and few if any of our daily responses to life are more likely to give pleasure to God—or on the other hand, distress—than the way we love. Jesus summed it up in a sweeping, challenging, life-encompassing statement: that we love God with everything that is in us, and that we love our neighbors as we love ourselves (which is a fascinating standard of judgment).

Now let's go from the sublime—love of God and neighbor—to the ridiculous (if you will allow me to use that word for something beloved by you). What shall we say about these daily elements to which we so often apply the verb *love*? What place does our dog, our canary, our car, our political affiliation, or our favorite restaurant, sports team, or performer have in this panoply of love?

Some will reply quickly and defensively that these subjects are quite different and that I'm asking to compare oranges with orangutans. Yes and no—because what gets our attention gets us. If while with spouse or friend or child we're thinking about work or politics or golf, it's right to ask what it is that we love. You want just now to remind me that if it were to come to a showdown, a life-and-death matter, there's no question which you love more. But here's our problem: all of life is a showdown. It's just that the showdown comes in a series of short episodes, episodes that are often so short and so casual that we don't grasp their eventual "showdown" quality.

So when work commitments break up families or political convictions end cherished friendships, or vacation spots become more important than human affection, we have to confess that our bumper-sticker loves are more powerful than we think. By virtue of the choices we make daily and even hourly, what seems like a careless use of the word *love* may be true beyond our realizing and beyond our willingness to acknowledge. Perhaps we really do love our pet, our team, our prevailing culture more than we love God or our neighbor. Perhaps this is because these bumper-sticker loves are more manageable than God or neighbor. We can close the door on the pet for an hour, not buy a season ticket this year, refuse the next appeal from our political cause. But God and the neighbor are with us always.

Love is not a convenience but a commitment. "Thou *shalt* love" runs counter to how we feel about love. Biblically, love is a commandment rather than an emotion, more a daily obligation than the satisfying of an inner longing. I do not love God or my neighbor because it is convenient (though it often is) or because they always appeal to me, but because they merit love. We don't always understand God or our neighbor. Sometimes they're flat out confusing, even irritating. They're not a convenience store for our needs, but an absolute essential for our fully human existence; as such, they lay claim on our whole being.

I smile each time I recall a wall motto in a secondhand bookstore; I wish I could give the author proper credit: "What I know about love is what a three-legged dog knows about automobiles." I suspect the author was referring to romantic love, but it applies just as well to any love worthy of the name. To love is to open ourselves to pain. The person, cause, or institution we love can fall short of our expectations—perhaps because our expectations are more than any person, cause, or institution can live up to or because the person dies, the cause fades, or the institution ceases to exist. To love is to invite sorrow.

Perhaps the noblest, most beautiful, and most powerful fact about love is that those who love know (or eventually learn) that loving is an exceedingly risky venture, yet they dare to love anyway.

God set the pattern. There surely is no more magnificent phrase in literature than "God so loved the world," and neither is there a more foolhardy one. The cynical student of history can give evidence that we humans just do one foolish thing after another. God seems therefore to have questionable taste in loving the world, and loving it with such abandon that *whosoever* can be saved. God would be a wiser investor if he were more selective. God goes to Eternity's racetrack and lays the divine ultimate on any and every horse in the race. Theologically, God bets the Lord Christ as much on the stumbling mongrel as the apparent thoroughbred.

We read that God is love, and looking at the track record of us humans we say, "How odd of God!" I suspect that the grand virtue of common sense would agree. If we were more Christlike, however, we would say, "How godly of God!"

So, God helping me, I intend to go on loving—people, causes, beauty, laughter, life, and love itself. And I'm altogether certain that however poor my judgment, God looks on with pleasure. Because God *is* love.

DAILY PROMISE

Today when I use the word *love* for some transient matter, I will ask myself how this love affects my commitment to what is eternal.

CHAPTER 14

MOVING

I come to this discussion with credentials of my own. I grew up in a time when homeowners were a minority in America. Renters are always at the mercy of the economy in general and of landlords in particular, so they tend to be movers. The major factor in our moving, however, was my mother. She dreamed of a day when the family would have "a little bungalow of our own," something that didn't happen until some years after I had left home. Meanwhile, she frequently noticed some rental property that for one reason or another seemed more attractive than the one in which we were currently living. So we moved—sometimes twice or more in a school year.

I didn't know it at the time, but we were in the best biblical tradition. Genesis tells us that when God created humanity, it was with the command to "fill the earth and subdue it" (Gen. 1:28). You can't fill the earth without some folks moving about. Some time later there was a problem at the place called Babel, when the people didn't want to be "scattered abroad." It was God's intention that the whole earth should be inhabited, and the people at Babel weren't cooperating. Divine judgment said they should move, and we humans have been moving ever since.

We are a migratory lot. Probably everyone who reads these words has moved at least once and more likely several times. Even more certainly, we are descended from people who moved. While there are thousands of small settlements across the world where people have lived isolated from any going or coming for more time than their records can tell, such settlements represent only a miniscule part of our human family. Virtually all of us have ancestors who moved across national boundaries, then across mountains and oceans to the places we now call home.

The moving hasn't stopped. Take the American scene. The latest data from the U.S. Census Bureau reports that over 14 percent of our population—almost exactly one in seven persons, for a total of 40,093,000 individuals— moved in the year of the last study. More than half of these moved within the same county. Many of these were either young families or individuals moving from a starter home to a more commodious setting, while others were downsizing from a family home to smaller quarters. Nearly 8 million moved from one county to another in the same state, and a slightly smaller number moved to a different state. And hear this: 1,269,000 moved to a different country. America has been a nation of movers from its earliest days. Once the covered wagon was the symbol of the frontier. Now the frontier is harder to identify, but the movers may operate with a nationwide moving company, by way of a rental truck, or with a trailer pulled by the traveler's automobile.

What is true in America is true all over the world. One of my former students is now pastor of an English-speaking congregation in a German city where on almost any Sunday her congregation includes persons from five continents. The whole world is on the move.

But statistics are not the issue, except as a sociological and economic study. Those who are moving are individuals, couples, or whole families, and to sum them up in millions and in percentages misses the point. Who are these people, and how are they affected by moving? How does it feel to move? What happens to a person's friendships, sense of belonging, or estimate of self-worth when they move? What happens to the bonds of family for those left behind and for those making the crucial transition together?

Not every move is a happy move. What shall we say for those millions who move to escape tyrants or political or religious persecution? And what of the hundreds of thousands who are displaced by famine or natural disaster? Who can measure the pain of those who spend years in displacement centers? They can't move physically, but who would dare to say that they are at home? They are nomads within walls, always moving but never going anywhere.

Many moves are the expression of dream fulfillment; people move to a dwelling place, an area of the country, or a position that has seemed for so long to be too good to be true. Sometimes, indeed, it proves to be. Only rarely, however, is a move so ideal that it doesn't involve elements of pain, especially when a spouse or another family member is involved. For one person the move is perfect, but for another family member it is simply accommodating to circumstances.

So much of the Bible is written by or about migrants. Abraham is the most notable figure in the Old Testament. He was the son of an adventuresome father, Terah, who left one of the great cities of its time, Ur of the Chaldees, to go to Canaan but died before arriving. Abraham finally picked up the journey when God spoke to him with a message that was simple beyond confusion: *Go. Leave country, family, and all that is familiar, and go.* As it turned out, he never really settled down, and the New Testament praises him for it. The writer of Hebrews says that Abraham went, "not knowing where he was going," and that in doing so he was setting an example for all of us, because those who follow in the spirit of Abraham "make it clear that they are seeking a homeland. If they had been thinking of the land that they had left behind, they would have had opportunity to return" (Heb. 11:8, 14–15).

Abraham's physical and spiritual descendants, the Israelites, moved to what they thought was a temporary residence in Egypt, but they ended up living there for four hundred years before becoming migrants again, moving to their land of promise by way of a generation-long wilderness. It seems that they never fully settled into that cherished home before a great number of them—the ten northern tribes—made an enforced move to Assyria, where they were assimilated into the nation that defeated them. A few generations later, the most wealthy, gifted, and prominent of the remaining body, Judah, moved (unwillingly) to Babylon. An anonymous member of that group has left us with one of the most poignant songs of an unintentional migrant, someone who has been moved against his will and who wants only to return home:

> By the rivers of Babylon—
> there we sat down and there we wept
> when we remembered Zion.
>
> (Ps. 137:1)

Nevertheless, it was during that time of living as a people on the move (in a captivity with which they would not make spiritual peace) that some of the prophets, such as Jeremiah and Ezekiel, and some reformers, such as Ezra and Nehemiah, made our Hebrew Scriptures richer. They managed to "sing the Lord's song / in a foreign land" (Ps. 137:4).

If the Old Testament is in so many ways the story of a people on the move, often written by persons on the move, the New Testament brings the theme forward in a new way. We have only a few stories of the people Jesus invited to be his disciples, but all were marked by the phrase, "Follow me." That is, get up and move! And for some who turned to Jesus with admirable idealism but were short on follow-through, Jesus had what seemed a sharp word: "Foxes have holes, and birds of the air have nests; but the Son of Man has nowhere to lay his head" (Matt. 8:20) —as if to make clear that to follow him meant to be on the move, with no certain dwelling place.

It's no wonder, then, that some of the most earnest followers of Jesus came to see themselves as pilgrims—that is, people on the move—yet confident of their ultimate destination even if they didn't possess a sure locale on this earth. The New Testament writer saw them as a restless people: "they are seeking a homeland." One needs accelerated vision to glimpse this homeland, but they know for sure that it is "a better country, that is, a heavenly one" (Heb. 11:14, 16).

There is for sure a restlessness in us human beings, whatever our religion or lack thereof. I vote with Augustine when he insists that our hearts are restless until they find their rest in God. It's no wonder that we are such inveterate movers. Nevertheless, I'm uneasy with folks who are so anxious for the world to come that they neglect this world. I believe with the first modern hymnist, Isaac Watts, that our present home "yields a thousand sacred sweets / before we reach the heavenly fields, / or walk the golden streets," and with that in mind that we will "let our songs abound, / and every tear be dry, / [since] we're marching through Emmanuel's ground / to fairer worlds on high."[1]

There's a restlessness in us human beings. As I read the Scriptures, at our best we have a double focus. With redeemed vision, we see the purposes of God for a redeemed kingdom on this earth. Beyond that we see a city "not made with hands, eternal in the heavens" (2 Cor. 5:1).

And as we live with both cities in view, we movers can believe that God finds pleasure in our moving. Because we're not just movers—we're pilgrims.

DAILY PROMISE

Today I will pray for and listen empathetically to someone who is coping with an unwanted or difficult move.

CHAPTER 15

ENTERTAINMENT

Thirty years ago, Neil Postman warned Americans with his book title that we were *Amusing Ourselves to Death*. Although Postman made his points in lively fashion, it was nevertheless a sober prediction. In his foreword he referred to Aldous Huxley's novel *Brave New World* (first published in 1932), which warned that for some future generation the greatest danger was not that books would be banned, as in another dystopian novel of the era, George Orwell's *1984*, but that truth would be drowned in "a sea of irrelevance."[1]

Postman wrote the book in 1985, when ESPN was only nine years old. Who would have imagined then that someday the National Football League would have its own channel, and so would the more powerful university athletic conferences. And who would have guessed that the time would come when we could watch old movies, classic television shows, golf, tennis, fishing, hunting, football, horse-racing, cooking, home remodeling—you name it—at any hour of the day or night. And what of the promise that a television set can make it possible for you to record five programs while you are watching a sixth? Hardly a person is now alive who remembers when most television and radio stations "signed off" every night, with a formula special to each. Aldous Huxley feared that what we desire might ruin us. Postman said we might be "amusing ourselves to death."

Has the quest for entertainment opened Pandora's box, to our ultimate destruction? Is the innocence another generation knew in listening to *Lux Radio Theater* now a monster that not only controls our time and our family life but is also our moral and cultural arbiter? If so, how can our use of it possibly bring pleasure to God? Is entertainment—a multibillion-dollar business—something that is beyond redemption and that will corrupt us to a point of no return? Have we, in fact, been so taken over by the desire for amusement that nothing else really matters?

Sometimes it's hard to tell the difference between an alarmist and a prophet. Of course, it's easy to make fun of an alarmist—and sometimes, as several of the Old Testament prophets might testify, it's easy to make fun of a prophet. That's what Amos and Jeremiah, among others, found so difficult about their work. Thus Jeremiah, with his words of doom, gave us a noun to describe a certain type of public address: *jeremiad:* "a lamentation; a mournful complaint." Are concerns about contemporary entertainment nothing but jeremiads?

I'm not as optimistic as I would like to be, and because I'm older than most, I recognize that I'm inclined to look back fondly on the simpler world of the "good old days," when there was entertainment but it was neither as intrusive, as culture-shaping, or as omnipresent as it is now. One of Billy Sunday's famous sermons was titled "Dancing, Drinking, and Card-Playing" (he was against them). If one were to preach against entertainment today, it would be a much longer sermon. In fact, the title itself might be interminably long.

I don't intend to attack entertainment as such. Whatever my concerns about the excesses of entertainment, I see it as a legitimate part of life. But even as I say that, I think of a classic and highly practical definition of sin — "legitimate desire drawn beyond legitimate bounds" — and I wonder, what are the God-given elements in entertainment? And how can our pleasure in entertainment, as performers or as receivers, bring pleasure to God?

I dare to think that entertainment is almost as native to human beings as our need for others, our instinct for language, and perhaps even our reach toward God. Some evangelists of my youth might have reasoned that the Eden story is, among other things, one of temptation to entertainment. I didn't hear such a theory, but I can imagine it. After all, the tempter helped our ancestors see that the fruit of the tree "was a delight to the eyes." It was not only "good for food" and something that would "make one wise," but it was wonderfully attractive; it looked like fun (Gen. 3:6). Well, that's entertainment!

The appetite is there. It's easy to imagine that as surely as medieval kings had a court jester, Abraham must have had among his more than three hundred workers some young man who did clever tricks with a camel, followed by a graceful bow, and then some older person in the entourage who could spin a half-historical, half-fanciful tale about their ancestors. Even the prophets knew how to entertain. When Jeremiah wanted to make a point for the king and his court, he did so by way of dramatically putting a yoke around his neck, and when a false prophet challenged him by breaking the yoke, Jeremiah replied with an iron yoke. The prophet was using entertaining, dramatic gifts to persuade. Jeremiah was not alone in this. The prophets often used dramatic devices to attract attention and to make their case. They knew that entertainment has its place. They employed it rather than deploring it.

But entertainment may well be as addictive as a physical drug. For some, entertainment is part of life, a form of leisure, or in some cases something like a hobby. For others, however, it consumes life until family, friends, God, and daily employment are pushed to the background. These are the persons who, if they were to lose their entertainment—cards, sports, music, gossip, television, movies, concerts—they would lose their reason for living. Entertainment can be as innocent and as beautiful as a grandparent reading nursery rhymes to a grandchild, or as destructive as parents who push their children aside so that they can pursue exotic vacations or watch their favorite television shows.

If entertainment has been part of our humanness for as long as we can remember, and if it has a legitimate place in life, what's good about it? Some would say that it depends on the nature of the entertainment, which is, of course, a cultural judgment shaped by our cultural convictions. I'm tempted to make such a case for reading, except that obviously not all reading material is good or worthy of our time. Some will make a case for music—*their* kind of music, that is. As for television, I confess to some strong opinions, but I must also confess that I didn't see the comedic artistry in *I Love Lucy* until long after it had gone into reruns. For some, their love of books or television is enhanced by a communal element—meeting in a book club or organizing a "watch party" so that friends can enjoy a favorite television show together.

The purpose of entertainment is to, well, *entertain.* Nevertheless, it is also clear that some entertaining is debasing. When the Roman amphitheaters became places where the entertainment succeeded only when it ended in gory death for animals, humans, or both, surely entertainment had become evil. It was consuming itself.

Most entertainment decisions are not so obvious. Take the matter of addiction, for instance. When does a hobby take over a life? When does listening to music isolate us from listening to persons? When does a cultural fascination with some period of history make us like Miniver Cheevy of poetry fame, who "wept that he was ever born" because he was captured by the past? When does some sport so take over life that we all but forget everything else? How often do we turn on the television to "see if there's something on tonight"? As one wise soul has said, there's always "something on." To what degree have we let entertainment in general or some particular form of it control our lives?

I suggest some questions to ask about entertainment: Does it leave me feeling better about life, more hopeful, or more challenged to make life better? Does it isolate me from humanity or draw me more thoughtfully into its circle? What makes me laugh, what do I find endearing, and what do I scorn? Do I laugh with pleasure at a comedian's masterful timing or with condescension at someone's peculiarity? What emotions does my favorite music raise in me? Does it make life larger and urge me to embrace more of life? What attitudes come from my reading? I enjoy certain essayists, but sometimes they leave me feeling superior to other people; is this a critique of the essays or the essayist, or of the state of my soul?

Entertainment should not be an escape from life, but a deeper, more real, more generous engagement in life. Entertainment is not heaven, because heaven will not be an eternal golf game or an unceasing performance by the New Jerusalem Symphony, but a fuller communion with God—and thus with my fellow humans.

Beyond doubt, entertainment can be misused. History is crowded with such stories. Just as surely, entertainment is an especially challenging issue in our day, as almost any thoughtful observer will confess. But the very capacity to entertain, and to receive entertainment, is a gift from our Creator, from our loving God. Rightly used, therefore, the pleasure we find in entertainment can please the God who gave us the capacity for its good and holy use.

DAILY PROMISE

Today I will examine two or three of my
favorite forms of entertainment to see
how they affect my total person.

CHAPTER 16

LEARNING

I grew up with mixed signals about learning, and now that I am old, I'm glad. I was born with a love of learning in my bones. This isn't a declaration of some superior endowment; rather, it's an announcement that I was born human. The capacity for learning varies dramatically from one person to another, and so too with the areas of learning that appeal to us and the methods by which we acquire knowledge. But the hunger to learn is surely as natural to a human as the hunger for food, for love, and for security. To be human is to be a learner.

Unfortunately, our culture teaches us to believe that learning is something that happens primarily (almost exclusively) through approved systems. In truth, learning goes on—for good and ill—whether or not those systems are at work. A child in an advantaged home learns about horticulture through the books her parents provide. The slave boy George Washington Carver learned about plants by tending them when his owner, Mr. Carver, chose to give him increasing freedom to exercise his extraordinary sensitivity to the world of soil and sunshine. One child learns to structure a sentence persuasively because he hears such speech in his home; another learns to be silent because when she speaks, she is ignored or reprimanded. Both are learning: one to fortune and the other to misfortune. Some learn early to trust, while others learn to be wary. Some learn that learning is power and joy and wonder, while others learn that to learn is to alienate yourself from your environment. We learn, even if for some it is learning not to learn.

My heritage, as I've indicated, was mixed. My parents had great regard for several of my older cousins who were educators or ministers, but they were skeptical if not scornful of those persons they felt "were educated beyond their intelligence." Given my circumstances, I saw learning very much at a pragmatic level; learning was good to the degree that it "worked," that it paid its way. I was older than most by the time I became a college student, and I still remember the adjunct professor in sociology who asked me excitedly, "Don't you find this concept fascinating?" I did, but I didn't know that it was a legitimate feeling. I was slow to realize that grasping a new idea can, in its own way, be as wonderful as discovering a continent.

Scholars have identified a substantial section of the Old Testament—from Job to Song of Solomon—as "wisdom literature." True, the psalms are poems of devotion and worship, but wisdom is woven throughout the prayers and calls to prayer. There is cynicism and life-weariness in Ecclesiastes, the song of a man who has so much of everything, including learning, that he questions the value of almost everything. But generally the books of wisdom are wonderfully practical, with a poetic lilt that makes one smile while learning.

The book of Job teaches its lessons in a setting of profound human pain, as a man who has lost everything but life itself reasons with well-meaning friends who have come to share with him their devastating "wisdom." One of the auxiliary lessons in the exchanges between Job and his friends is that even very wise people speak from their own prejudices and can therefore be wrong—or at the least, not very helpful. As the story concludes, God rebukes Job's friends for the failure of their reasoning. It was a failure that perhaps had more to do with their unwillingness to empathize. If their hearts had been more open to Job's pain, they would have heard him better— which is to say, the willingness to listen with one's whole being is itself high wisdom.

Aristotle said, "To learn is a natural pleasure, not confined to philosophers, but common to all men." For that reason, it is also true that we can learn from almost anyone. We would learn more if we entered situations with a readiness to learn. Sometimes learning becomes its own worst enemy in that the person who has studied extensively in some field reads a book, attends a lecture, or enters a discussion defensively, expecting that all he encounters will be old stuff to him. Thus, he closes the door of learning.

The world of the Internet, of smartphones, and of who-knows-what-else-before-this-book-reaches-your hands is changing the very face of learning. I think of a story from half a century ago in which some African workers, seeing their missionaries write information in their notebooks, spoke of white people as "carrying their brains in their pockets." Many Africans, unable to write, developed prodigious memories—no doubt more effective memories than those of the educated missionaries. Are we humans coming to a place where information will be so easily available on a variety of gadgets that it will no longer be necessary to "learn" all the things that once were indispensable?

If that be so, what will it do to creativity? Will we abandon musical composition, the writing of essays, and laboratory research to handheld devices? If so, what might happen to the human brain? A gift unused is, in time, a gift lost. If it becomes so easy to produce mechanized art, music, and literature, will the creative person become as scarce as the person who knits a sweater or as those who choose to cook from scratch? Will creativity become a hobby available only to those who have the time and desire to enjoy it? And then, what kind of persons will we become? Will we lose our ability to learn, since there's no need to learn when all knowledge is available at our fingertips? Or will all of us become skilled machine operators, who know which buttons to press or which commands to give to our voice-sensitive gadgets so that they will think for us?

I can't imagine such a world, but when I was a boy reading a comic strip about Buck Rogers in the twenty-fifth century, I couldn't have believed that I would someday watch humans landing on the moon. Whatever the gains in more easily accessible knowledge, I cherish the wonder of learning. I want always to see in someone's eyes the light I saw in the eyes of the sociology professor when she spoke of the excitement of a concept. It is a profound privilege to learn. And with Aristotle, I rejoice in learning as a natural pleasure that is available to all persons.

Over six hundred years ago a Jewish scholar said, "Who does not learn, cannot truly love God."[1] Since God has blessed us human creatures with that computer beyond all computers, the human mind, it is silent blasphemy to leave the mind undeveloped. If God is the ultimate intelligence, how can one love God without loving learning? If, as Jesus said, the first commandment is to love God with all our heart, soul, and mind, then the better our mind, the better equipped we are to love God.

Many of us smile in agreement with Winston Churchill's confession: "Personally, I'm always ready to learn, although I do not always like being taught."[2] One of the substantial benefits of learning is that it requires humility. Learning begins by confessing that someone knows more than we do. That person learns best and most who approaches the teacher most humbly. This doesn't mean turning off our critical facilities, because learning demands discernment, but it begins with the posture of humility, the realization that we don't know it all. Perhaps, indeed, we know very little, and the grandest moment of learning is when we realize how much more there is to learn.

Today, learning is literally at our fingertips. We can touch an instrument we hold in our hands and lay hold of information from every corner of the world and from any age of history. Our greatest problem now is discrimination between what is worth knowing and what is of little value or perhaps even destructive; for sometimes knowledge is cannibalistic, eating its own best creations. So love is changed to pornography, and science to annihilation. With so much learning available, what learning is to be prized above all other, and where can it be found?

Before the time of well-staffed, multimillion-dollar laboratories and brilliant assistants, George Washington Carver did his miracles. Carver told his friends at Tuskegee Institute how he did his work: "First, I go into the woods and gather specimens, and listen to what God has to say to me. After I have had my morning talk with God, I go to my laboratory and begin to carry out His wishes for the day, and if I fail it's my failure, and if I succeed then God's will has been done."[3]

Carver was a lifelong learner, beginning as a slave boy near Diamond Grove, Missouri. I'm sure that as Carver learned and then worked his miracles with peanuts and sweet potatoes and the very soil of a riverbed, he felt God's pleasure. We can too.

DAILY PROMISE

Today I will ask myself what I can learn from a particular person who seems less endowed, less formally educated, or less imaginative than I perceive myself to be.

CHAPTER 17

SOLITUDE

Solitude may be the item in shortest supply in the values market of our postmodern world. This is partly because our world is becoming more and more urban, which means that we are crowding people together ever more insistently, and with them the "sounds" of people. It's also because we're working longer hours. This is contrary to the predictions of a decade or two ago, when people envisioned a lighter workload, thanks to new technologies, which probably makes it all the more difficult for us to cope with what is happening.

The more particular problem, however, is that solitude is an art. It doesn't happen automatically when we have spare time or no people are around; we have to commit ourselves to it intentionally. Very few of us seem to know how to pursue solitude—or worse, to recognize it when it's thrust on us. How many people have you heard say, "I'd just like to have some time to myself!" before getting into their automobile (one of the most secluded spots on the planet) and immediately turning on the radio to listen to the voices of musicians or announcers—or worse (because of the hazards involved), texting. We think we want to be alone, but we don't recognize the opportunities when they thrust themselves on us.

A small but growing number of persons are turning to retreats, some in search of God and some simply in search of quiet. Some have chosen monasteries where speech is forbidden. But a weekend isn't enough for the harried soul. Solitude is at its best when we build it into the continuing pattern of time rather than as an occasion. A weekend retreat can be life transforming, as many testify, but if it is truly to be that, solitude must be a value system and a commitment rather than simply an event.

Before I go further, let me also say that solitude is not necessarily good of itself. We can misuse it, like any other human experience. Russian novelist Vladimir Nabokov wrote, "Solitude is the playfield of Satan."[1] If you've read Nabokov, you know that he had a sophisticated sense of evil—of its power, its subtlety, and its presence in the general fabric of life. Solitude is powerful, and it can be powerful for evil as well as for good. There's something of this idea in the ancient belief that demons especially inhabited the wilderness, the place of enforced solitude; hence a term we still use: the howling wilderness.

Remember, too, that loneliness is not the same thing as solitude. We can long for solitude, but it's hard to imagine someone wanting to feel lonely. But as surely as one can be lonely in the midst of a crowd (as most of us know, a crowd is sometimes the loneliest of places), so too one can learn to find solitude in the midst of a crowd, though it takes a concentrated effort to do so.

The longing for solitude is not necessarily a longing for God or for a reality beyond ourselves. Solitude can in fact be a sophisticated expression of ego: we want to be alone because we find no other company as satisfying as our own. We may have arguments within ourselves, but at least we respect the source of the contrary opinions, since the source is within our own singular person. Ego, indeed!

Nevertheless, the place of solitude is a place of potential, unique beauty. God, being God, could have spoken to Moses anywhere, but we're not surprised that God spoke to this great soul in a place of solitude. It seems likely that other, younger shepherds were assisting Moses in tending what was no doubt a large flock of sheep, but there was plenty of open space between the workers, and hours on end when a human voice was heard only occasionally or other persons seen only at a distance. And it was not only that Moses was alone when God spoke but that he had spent years in such daylong and sometimes nightlong stretches of aloneness. A poet, novelist, or dramatist imagines the conversations Moses carried on within his own soul and perhaps with God prior to the ecstatic moment when God called, "Moses, Moses!"

Nor is it incidental that the Spirit led Jesus into the wilderness after his baptism. Jesus' baptism was a triumphant moment. John the Baptist celebrated it by introducing Jesus as the Lamb of God who would bear the sins of the world, after which "a voice from heaven said, 'This is my Son, the Beloved, with whom I am well pleased'" (Matt. 3:17). Then the Spirit led Jesus into the wilderness, into a place of testing. And for forty days and nights he fasted in solitude and faced insidious temptation.

That most extraordinary of books, Revelation, came to its author while he was imprisoned on the island of Patmos, "because of the word of God and the testimony of Jesus" (Rev. 1:9). I suppose he could have received God's message in Rome; this might have been appropriate, since part of the message dealt with a great city of commerce, which was almost surely Rome. But it's hard to imagine the out-of-this-world visions of Revelation coming in any place other than utter solitude. One would need acute spiritual hearing to grasp such complexity, such grandeur, such ultimate triumph of goodness. Only solitude would do.

Octavio Paz calls solitude "the profoundest fact of the human condition." He contends, further, that "man is the only being who knows he is alone."[2] We humans are self-conscious creatures; we examine ourselves and internalize our experiences. Thus, so many of humanity's highest moments of self-understanding and of God-seeking have come at times of solitude.

Nevertheless, solitude frightens many—indeed, it frightens all of us if we wonder how long or how deep the experience might be. It's no wonder that solitary confinement is seen as the worst punishment short of the death penalty. When we hear that victims of international conflict are being held in solitary confinement for months and even years, we wonder how they keep their sanity and if the experience leaves emotional and mental wounds that will never heal.

Still, we need to be alone. We need time to become acquainted with ourselves at levels that are impossible when others are around. When Laurie Haller, a United Methodist minister, was awarded a three-month retreat from a Lilly Endowment grant, she wanted especially to be alone. She had been an effective pastor in a good-size parish and also an administrative officer in her denomination. She was a dedicated wife (her husband is also a parish pastor) and mother. But she had grown weary of the constant pressure of people and of seemingly unceasing demands on her time, so the purpose of her extended retreat was solitude. As the period drew to a close, she observed, "Solitude gave me the space to see how arrogant, presumptuous, and manipulative I often am in my conversation."[3]

Haller's honesty is unnerving because it makes me wonder what I might learn about myself if I had an extended period of solitude. But it also authenticates her solitude: she was becoming acquainted with parts of herself that there was no time to know when she was busy. This is not to suggest, however, that solitude will bring only self-condemnation. I think of some people who live with verbal abuse or forms of belittlement. In solitude, such a person may well hear a voice that says, "You're much better than you realize, you know."

An eminently practical person might see something pretentious in the person who expresses a need for solitude. "I need time to be alone" can seem egotistical, and "I want time alone with God" may appear the height of egotism — who do we think we are that we should have a private audience with the Almighty? But in truth, who else on this planet is it more important that we should know with clarity than our own soul? And in the issues of eternity, who more than God? The Bible makes clear that God considers us humans worth knowing. Few if any come away from an encounter with God impressed with their own importance. Their uniqueness, yes, and their holy potential, but not their importance above the person down the street or across the breakfast table. Indeed, it's blasphemous to think that a meeting with God would cause others to diminish in our sight.

If it is true that solitude is especially difficult to get in our time and if it is true (as the Scriptures and centuries of human experience suggest) that God desires to commune with us humans, then the loveliest frontier of human need may be our need of solitude. And perhaps nothing would give the God of the ages more pleasure than if we allowed the Holy Spirit to lead us into places of holy solitude.

DAILY PROMISE

Today I will embrace opportunities for
solitude, resisting the urge to fill the
space and silence with distractions.

CHAPTER 18

WALKING

A score or more years ago as I contemplated growing older, I asked myself what pleasures of life it would be hardest to give up. Two came immediately to mind: seeing and hearing. But the third was not far behind: walking. I realized that one of the great pleasures of my life was walking and the opportunity it gave for contemplation.

I'm speaking of the act itself, not the attendant health benefits. I'm secretly grateful that jogging and exercise walking came into vogue when I was too old to begin — or so I reasoned. But walking, and the mental and spiritual joys that come with it, is a gift beyond measure. This is true whether one is walking alone with thoughts (or even without them) or with a friend and his thoughts. Such walking was a gift I wanted to cling to as long as possible.

Then one morning, in a hurry and inattentive to black ice under a dusting of snow, I fell and broke the ball in my right hip. The orthopedic surgeon did his work well, but walking was never quite the same. Now I was conscious of the mechanics. Walking was drawing attention to itself. Previously walking had provided the accompaniment for a variety of other pleasures: thinking, praying, talking to a friend or to myself, observing life, reveling in trees and grass and sometimes snow, smiling at God; all of these are among the vast wonders of being alive that are best observed while walking. I still walk, but with less pleasure—and increasingly, of course, with more care.

But I believe in walking as much as I ever did. I'm glad I walked to school—not the interminable distances to which some testify, but always half a mile or more. And I'm glad for work that required me to walk. I'm glad for the walking I did in New York City during the six months I lived there: so many times from Columbus Circle to Times Square, then back to Central Park.

I have had friends for whom walking demanded so much more than it did for me. Long ago there was Casimir; a birth illness had left him crippled so that every step he took demanded painful cooperation from his whole body. There were others with canes and crutches, and several for whom a wheelchair makes locomotion possible. I honor these persons for capturing the walk experience when it takes such a marked effort to do so.

I'm an ordinary walker. I know there are impressive physical benefits in walking, but to learn about them you'll have to turn elsewhere. I'm not opposed to such benefits. Sometimes they come to mind when I'm talking, and sometimes they prod me when I'm sitting at my desk, to tell me how good it would be if I'd get up and walk. But I'm not presenting a lesson in physical culture. Nor do I have the instincts of the great Maimonides, the twelfth-century rabbi, physician, and philosopher, who said that one can tell by a person's walk whether he is wise and intelligent or foolish and ignorant. Maimonides lived in a culture where walking was more utilitarian than it is today. People walked to get where they needed to be; perhaps this made their walking more revealing of character. Did Maimonides see something as obvious as a slouching walk versus a purposeful stride? Was there something in a person's length of stride, the carriage of the body, or the tilt of the head that revealed the wisdom or the foolishness of the walker? We can only imagine.

Walking gets an early place in the Bible, and it involves God rather than humans. I wouldn't build a doctrine around it, but I'm impressed that as Genesis reports it, God's first activity following the completion of creation and some instructions to Adam and Eve was "walking in the garden at the time of the evening breeze" (Gen. 3:8). I realize that the Bible is speaking poetically, but I think the wording is significant and instructive. I like the hour, too: "the time of the evening breeze." That's the time another generation called "the gloaming," the time to be lonely (almost happily so) and the time to ponder the purposes of life, the importance of relationships, and the challenge to make more of tomorrow than we've made of today. It's good to walk any time, but early in the day or near the end of its daylight hours are especially auspicious times.

Again, while I wouldn't build a doctrine around it, I am impressed that one of the most prominent of Jesus' postresurrection appearances involves two persons who were walking. We have the name of only one, Cleopas, and we know nothing more about him beyond his name. We discern that the two were earnest believers and that they were devastated by the death of their Lord and mystified by what they had heard thus far about his resurrection. But as they walked, Jesus appeared to them. It happened while they were walking and doing what friends and associates so often do while walking: they were talking. I'm confident that a great many of us have had some of our best conversations with God while walking, because our spiritual hearing is often better then.

Nowadays people often walk for a cause, either as demonstrators in a march or as persons pledged to raise money for a charity. Some walk to be alone, and some walk to enjoy a friend. Some gladly greet you while they walk, while others make it clear that if you speak to them you will intrude on their privacy. Some smile while they walk, not intentionally but because they're enjoying themselves. Others seem to be coping with some deep, inner anger that compels them to tramp on resolutely with every step. Some walk fast, some slowly, some determinedly with a cane. Almost never do I see someone walk with a flourish, like Fred Astaire, celebrating the world as his oyster.

This is to say that walking is for every mood, with purpose or without, alone or with someone—and sometimes alone even while with someone. In America we don't do much walking to get somewhere, except from our parking space to the store or church or office. When we inquire of a storekeeper in England about a church, a building, or a landmark, we may hear that it's "just a ten-minute walk"—and we learn to add several minutes to the estimate because the British walk faster than we do. If we were back in America we would say, "Let's just jump in the car. We can get there in a minute or two."

We need to reclaim walking as part of life—not as an exercise, not for an occasional cause, but as part of life itself. The ancient figure of speech is wiser than we realize. God walked in the garden; he didn't fly in or drop by for a visit. Enoch's remarkable biography is in four short verses, but the writer speaks the key element twice— "Enoch *walked* with God"—before announcing his remarkable exit: "then he was no more, because God took him" (Gen. 5:21–24). The psalmist has us walk through the valley of the shadow, not run nor stumble (Ps. 23:4). Paul talks several times about running, but his basic figure of speech for the Christian life is walking. Bunyan's pilgrim made his progress while he walked.

Walking is still our basic mode of transportation, though many of us in the urban world don't think so. After all, it's walking that gets us from one room in our home or apartment to another, and from one location in our place of work to the next. One of the early reports of recovery after a medical emergency is still the ability to walk.

But where we are different from even our ancestors is that we don't walk distances of any length out of doors unless by intention. And it is in the longer walks that we are more likely to breathe deeply, both physically and spiritually. This is a reward that we need intentionally to regain. As John Updike—poet, novelist, essayist, and literary award winner—noted near the end of his autobiography, *Self-Consciousness,* those who are older discover that "even a walk to the mailbox is a precious experience, that all species of tree and weed have their signature and style and the sky is a pageant of clouds." Updike returns to the figure of speech in the last sentence of the book: "The self's responsibility, then, is to achieve rapport, if not rapture with the giant, cosmic other: to appreciate, let's say, the walk back from the mailbox."[1]

That's what Enoch did, sublimely, obviously in a class by himself. He walked with God, and God *took* him. I'm certain that if you and I learned to walk better—more attentively to God and wonder and life, and with more gratitude—we would now and again be taken by God.

To God's pleasure.

DAILY PROMISE

Today I will walk attentively and gratefully.
Whether from room to room, from parking lot
to destination, or while exercising, I will cherish
the ability to move, and I will thank God.

CHAPTER 19

READING

It is unwise to begin a chapter or an address with an apology, but I'm compelled to do so just now. I love reading too much to do justice to it. Nevertheless, it's impossible for me to write a book about giving pleasure to God without including reading. Reading has given me so much pleasure for so many years that I can't imagine giving pleasure to God and omitting reading.

How much do I love reading? When I make my annual pilgrimage to my hometown of Sioux City, Iowa, I visit the sites of all the schools I attended, all the houses I lived in, the two churches that nurtured my young faith, and the libraries—three of them. One was the central library, where I spent so many hours doing research for my high school debate team; it is now an apartment building for retirement living. The second is a neighborhood library where I got my first library card; it is now a place of grass, part of a small neighborhood park. The third, too, was a neighborhood library, where I reveled in so many happy summer afternoons of my twelfth and thirteenth years; it is now a neighborhood community house of some sort. All three are like shrines for me. As I visit them, I reminisce, embrace them with my heart, and thank God for public libraries and for books.

The book that has influenced me most is the Bible. I've read it through, Genesis to Revelation, dozens of times, beginning when I was eleven years old. So what does the Bible say about reading? The word appears often, beginning in Exodus and continuing into Revelation. In the Old Testament, reading was a community enterprise, partly because not many persons could read and even fewer could possess anything resembling what today we call books.

The occasions of these public readings were momentous. The Lord had spoken to Moses, as the slave people Israel was coming to birth as a nation, and Moses in turn "wrote down all the words of the Lord." Here is the principle of a book, or even of a periodical: if by one means or another we have received words that we think are worth preserving, we inscribe them so that they won't be lost. As a result, we have written records dating back more than four thousand years. (By contrast, it's barely a century that we've been able to make a vocal recording. And what's worse, in that brief time the recording process has changed so steadily and so dramatically that media used for such recordings become outdated within a decade or two!)

As for Moses and his message, the morning after writing down the words, Moses prepared a sacred setting, with pillars representing the twelve tribes, and there "he took the book of the covenant, and read it in the hearing of the people" (Exod. 24:4, 7). When I read of the twelve-pillar setting Moses made for his public reading, I think of Machiavelli, who in evenings of solitude would dress as if he were entertaining dinner guests before reading the authors he revered most. Great reading deserves some such grandeur.

Centuries later, when the remnants of Israel were returning from the captivity of Babylon and Persia, again there was a community reading from the covenant book: "Ezra opened the book in the sight of all the people, for he was standing above all the people, and when he opened it, all the people stood up." As Ezra read, a team of thirteen Levites stood ready to answer questions. Ezra's assistants "gave the sense, so that the people understood the reading" (Neh. 8:5, 8). It was neither a formality nor a magic performance; it was a time of learning and of recommitment to the holy covenant. And it came by reading from a book.

With this heritage, the Jews became known as the people of the Book; so too did the Christians. The book carried the faith from one generation to another, giving its teachers the basic document for their work. So the faith was communicated to succeeding generations. We owe it to books, with their medium of an animal's hide or papyrus and something resembling ink that the message was preserved for generations to come.

But if you think this is simply the narrow prejudice of a religious advocate, there is more to the story. It is books that have preserved language, and with it general definitions of meaning, making intelligent discussion possible through generations. Without books, languages depend on the ear to carry words from one generation to another and on personal memory to define their meaning. See what happened with the Bible. Luther's translation of the Bible established the German language for that ethnic group, just as later the King James, or Authorized Version, did for the English language. Around the world, literally hundreds of language groups have their native tongue in written form because Christian missionaries converted oral language into written characters so that they could give people the Bible, or large portions of it. In the seventeenth century, New England was the most literate society in the world at the time because the people wanted their children to be able to read the Bible and other literature. Larry Witham describes their reading material: "Published sermons out-numbered almanacs, newspapers, and political pamphlets four to one."[1] It was a reading nation, and of religious literature especially.

But reading is not a virtue of itself. Like all human pursuits, reading can be used for good or for ill, to build or to destroy. Reading can be a vehicle for pornography and for disseminating philosophies of hate. *Mein Kampf* was a major instrument in Hitler's campaign of malice. Unfortunately, Hitler was neither the first nor the last to use books as systems for hate or destruction. Even great books have been twisted to such ends. Those of us who cherish the Bible confess that over the centuries many have used portions of it to hurt or control others. As one who loves reading, I rejoice when someone tells me that their daughter or son loves books. Then questions rise in my mind: What is the child reading? Will it lead to a generous, redemptive spirit or to a sense of superiority? Will it challenge the mind and character or simply preoccupy it? Since reading is so powerful, it isn't surprising that some want to censor it. And I suspect that no thinking person will deny that the wrong kind of reading can do great harm. Thus, it is important that a child learn not only to read but also to develop a sense of taste. I continue to subscribe to a statement I learned long ago: we should be exposed to the very best so that we will be able in time to recognize what is better.

And how do we know what is best? Or who shall decide? At the least, books should enlarge our lives rather than diminishing them, and they should make us hunger for virtue rather than vice. We know that something is not good if it makes us hateful, mean-spirited, or unkind to others. Good reading makes us sympathetic toward those we don't know rather than fearing or despising them. Good reading increases our vocabulary because it teaches us to know the difference between the right word and the almost-right word. And good reading should draw us closer to God.

Almost a generation ago, the Russian poet Joseph Brodsky received the Nobel Prize for Literature. In his acceptance speech, he said that in the history of our human race "the book is an anthropological development similar essentially to the invention of the wheel," that it "constitutes a means of transportation through the space of experience at the speed of a turning page."[2] Brodsky's love of reading and of books came at a price. He was expelled from his home country because of his books—a commutation of a sentence of five years at hard labor. In time he became an American citizen, and in 1991–1992, he served as poet laureate of the United States.

Dictators of any kind—political, religious, or intellectual—always fear the power of reading. This is a high tribute to reading's power and value. Can it be misused? Without a doubt. I know of no virtue, no beauty, no gift of God or of nature that cannot be misused. I have long believed, however, that truth has nothing to fear in the field of fair and open battle. This is perhaps the strongest argument for God finding pleasure in our reading. Not only does the act of reading exercise our minds and fuel our imagination, but it celebrates the freedom of the human conscience to seek knowledge and insight wherever it may be found, trusting that God's truth will always prevail.

As surely as reading has always been a hazard to those who fear it, many today feel that reading is in danger of what we fondly call progress. They say that radio and recordings have made us a more auditory people and that television has inclined us to the graphic, such that we read less and less, slowly returning to the state of the caveman carving pictures on the wall.

If that hazard lies in our future, I shall turn to the God of Moses and Ezra, who read to the people of God, and to God's poets and prophets, who left us with the Holy Scriptures, and I will pray that if God finds pleasure in our reading, it will be divinely protected for generations still to come.

DAILY PROMISE

Today I will begin reading selectively. I will ask myself what books or periodicals I would read if I knew that my reading days were limited—because, of course, they are.

CHAPTER 20

SHOPPING

My wife, Janet, doesn't read my books unless and until they're published. She will be surprised to find that this book includes a chapter on shopping and that I think shopping might bring pleasure to God.

Even if I'm not myself much of a shopper, I know that shopping is an important factor in life as most of us live it today. Indeed, this has been so for a very long time. With only a little imagination, we can see that one of the earliest scenes in the book of Genesis involves a purchase. The seller never mentioned the price; that little detail came later. And for that matter, Adam and Eve (like many innocent shoppers) didn't even realize they were in the market for a purchase until it was too late. They were only window-shopping in the marvels of their garden when they learned there was something they didn't have — and in that moment they became shoppers. And buyers!

It seems that we've been shopping ever since. How much? In this, as in so many matters, we have plenty of statistics. A survey of British buyers reports that Britons spend a total of 444 hours a year shopping; that's 18.5

days, or more than half a month. On average the British spend two hours a week grocery shopping, two hours shopping for clothing, and the remainder shopping for all other items.[1]

According to another survey, Americans invest 3.5 hours a week in shopping. The average is much higher in America's largest cities, ranging from 3.9 hours a week in Phoenix all the way to 6.5 hours a week in Chicago and 7 hours a week in New York City.[2] And of course there are other factors: How much time do shoppers spend driving to the mall or the supermarket? How long do some stand in line for the latest smartphone or some other device? Joshua Becker, who pleads for a culture where we "live more by owning less," says that we should also add in the time we spend in cleaning, sorting, and organizing our purchases after we've returned home.[3] He has a point.

The shopping scene keeps changing. Those who read English novels know there was a time when every village had a grocer, a fruiter, a butcher, and a baker. Then all these were put under one roof. In our day, the supermarket also includes a pharmacy as well as items of furniture and clothing. The downtown our American ancestors knew included a variety of clothing stores and other specialty shops. These morphed into the department store and then into the shopping mall. Predictors tell us that the shopping mall itself may soon struggle for life, because 55 percent of American shoppers prefer to shop online.[4] No one can say how our grandchildren or great-grandchildren will shop, but almost surely they will do so. Unless the world economy completely collapses, they will probably shop with more choices and be presented with more insistent voices and more clever devices than we can imagine today.

It's interesting the way shopping reinvents itself. In a sense, there's little new about Internet shopping—at least, not in its broader outlines. After all, several generations of Americans, especially in rural areas and small towns, waited anxiously for a catalog from Sears Roebuck, Spiegel's, or

Montgomery Ward. Such a catalog brightened endless winter evenings. There was something for every member of the family and for every occasion, from the toolbox in the barn to the dress for the annual box social. And while television's shopping channels and infomercials seem to have an impossible edge on a catalog, catalogs haven't lost their appeal. You have evidence of that every few days when some new catalog finds its way into your mailbox. The catalog retains its appeal because it allows you to ponder the possibilities unhurried, to know the quality of the seller, and to feel that the decision is yours rather than something pressed on you.

We're possessed by a spirit of acquisition. A street-corner philosopher or theologian might contend that Eden's original sin was simply the desire (in the midst of perfection!) to have something *more*. Certainly if there had been another garden next to Eden, the original shoppers would have gone there, too.

But shoppers don't deserve an altogether bad name. One of the most lauded persons in the Bible was a shopper, an expert one. What's more, she was endorsed by an iconic wise man. You'll find the report in the book of Proverbs, in what is sometimes called "An Ode to a Capable Wife." It begins, "A capable wife who can find? / She is far more precious than jewels," and it continues from there to list the virtues that make her so exemplary. Among them is shopping:

> She seeks wool and flax,
> and works with willing hands.
> She is like the ships of the merchant,
> she brings her food from far away.
> (Prov. 31:10, 13–14)

This admirable woman is no casual shopper. She doesn't buy at the first market in the bazaar or following her initial visit to a real estate agent. She doesn't hesitate to go "far away" to find the food she thinks is appropriate for her family. As for a field—obviously a major purchase—she "considers" the land before buying it (Prov. 31:16).

The woman in the proverb demonstrates that there is shopping, and then there is *shopping*. Some may give it a bad name, but this is not to deny its possible and proper virtue. It can be such a virtue, in fact, that Jesus chose a shopper as the hero of a parable: "Again, the kingdom of heaven is like a merchant in search of fine pearls; on finding one of great value, he went and sold all that he had and bought it" (Matt. 13:45).

When Jesus looks for a way to describe the kind of people who finally gain the kingdom of heaven, he finds his example in a merchant who is a specialist in quality, one who knows the difference between a pearl and a faux pearl—indeed, the difference between a beautiful pearl and an exquisite, once-in-a-lifetime kind of pearl. This man shops relentlessly, tirelessly, visiting one pearl dealer after another. Sometimes he almost gives up the search; at other times he almost decides to take something below his best vision. This kind of person, Jesus said—this inveterate, passionate shopper—is the kind of person who will at last find the kingdom of heaven. Such people won't settle for bargain-counter piety or a synthetic imitation; they won't be content with religion that looks acceptable as long as no one puts it to too deep a test. Such are the people who will make the kingdom, the people who will sell all that they have in order to get it.

I think about this pearl seeker sometimes when I recall conversations from my pastoral days. When we pastors would meet, sometimes one would say, "A new family attended our church recently: the Gibsons. Seemed like nice people." At that point, two colleagues would smile and then would note that the Gibson family had been in each of their churches for six months or a year. And then the diagnosis: "I'm afraid they're just church shoppers."

Years later, I wonder what kind of shoppers those people were. Perhaps they were the worst kind: people looking for a bargain faith, something that would fill an occasional gap in their social or community life. But might they have been master shoppers, like the pearl seeker in Jesus' parable, passionately seeking a faith that was worth selling out to, while our churches were offering unholy mediocrity? So they kept looking and kept being disappointed. If so, the shoppers are not to be blamed but rather those offering inferior products.

Shopping can be an end in itself, but it may be an expression of economic necessity for someone who watches every penny so that the family's needs can be met. It can also be a quality of judgment, as exemplified by the honored woman of Proverbs who knew the difference between the wool and the flax put forward by the several merchants, or as demonstrated by the person of earnest judgment who shops the television, movie, or literary opportunities and decides there's little there that is worthy of her highest possession: time. Shopping as a means of expressing good judgment is seen especially in the shopper for truth, who seeks eternal quality in the midst of this year's fads.

Our God is a God of excellence. I dare therefore to think that when God sees some of his discerning humans shopping to find that which is authentic and worth the price (however that price may be measured), God finds pleasure in their shopping. But God's bar of judgment is high.

DAILY PROMISE

Today I will ask myself what products,
ideas, or occasions deserve my attention and
resources. I will shape my shopping in the
pattern of the wise woman of Proverbs and
the pearl-seeking hero of Jesus' parable.

CHAPTER 21

GREEN GRASS
AND ASPHALT

The title of this chapter is meant to be neither cynical nor clever, just realistic. Two quite different poets played a part in creating the title. Playing off Joyce Kilmer's "I think that I shall never see / a poem lovely as a tree,"[1] Ogden Nash united trees and billboards and concluded, "Unless the billboards fall / I'll never see a tree at all."[2] And there's T. S. Eliot, who described his generation as one whose "only monument the asphalt road / And a thousand lost golf balls."[3]

We live in a world where nature and antinature have collided, and nature is struggling to hold its share, even though it was here first. I've used the term *antinature* because it has so many faces. Commerce is one, certainly, and progress is another. So too is population growth; with humanity numbering in the billions, green grass is inevitably being replaced by asphalt. "That's progress," an investor or a bigger-is-better enthusiast says as acres of farmland become a shopping mall. A few years later, when a new mall a mile away makes the previous one a collection of "for rent" signs and marginal businesses, I reply cynically, "So that's progress, is it?"

I love nature, but my love is unsophisticated. My definition of a perfect place to work is a room with abundant bookcases and a window that looks out on trees. I have such, but as I pause just now to look at the trees, I admit that I have no idea what kind of trees I'm seeing. I love the cycle of nature that will operate in the tree over the year, but I don't have a name for the tree. My ignorance embarrasses me, as it should. My public confession relieves my shame just a little.

Because I cherish nature, I get uneasy with efforts to improve on it. Our home has trees in back and front, and the backyard slopes gently into a pond. It's a small pond, but a real pond, left over from when this was farmland. They tell me there are fish, but no one fishes here. Each morning as I eat breakfast looking out on this little bit of nature, I give thanks with my eyes open: for the trees, for the pond, for the grass where I vow often to sit but rarely do.

I'm troubled, though, because my neighbor across the pond has tried to beautify nature by building a low stone wall where his property borders the pond. Mind you, it's an attractive bit of masonry, well done and not too high. Nevertheless, for me it is what another poet, the late nineteenth-century English priest Gerard Manley Hopkins, called an *inscape*, an intrusion on nature. Hopkins believed that our world "is charged with the grandeur of God" but that "generations have trod, have trod" so that now "all is seared with trade"[4] and we have lost our ability to grasp its wonder.

Hopkins wrote those words in 1877. What would he say today, as day after day, unceasingly, we feed thousands of acres of grass, wildflowers, cropland, and orchards into the insatiable maw of progress? Father Hopkins was a person of faith; he believed nevertheless that "the Holy Ghost over the bent / World broods with warm breast and with ah! bright wings."[5] I wonder if, in this twenty-first century, he could still hope that the Holy Spirit would speak to us humans through the untamed loveliness of God's creation? Would he hear the voice of God still, in the asphalt?

You and I seem to have limited choice. The asphalt is taking over daily. And I'm part of the process; most of us are. I mentioned that where I live was once farmland. The same can be said for most of us. Go back far enough and it's true of all of America; a few centuries ago, the land was farm, hunting ground, or wilderness. Now we move from the city to the suburbs, and from the suburbs to the exurbs. While we move to new settings where we can have more grass and carefully nurtured, civic-board-approved trees, we add to the asphalt and empower it more forcefully. At vacation time we look for nature: a week at a lake, a trip to a national park, or picnics in a city park. As we do so, we leave our environmental footprint via the gas used by automobile or airplane. But our souls need it. Something of our Eden memory wants to reclaim a garden in the cool of the day. Not too carefully manicured, not even too helpfully marked—we seek just a place where the Maker somehow seems near at hand. Some live close enough to nature that in a few steps or a few miles there's a measure of solitude. Others build a small garden in the window of a skyscraper apartment. Still others vacation at the shore. We all seem to crave the grass, not the asphalt.

The book of Genesis makes an implicit case against cities. Humanity's idyllic opening scene is a garden. Then came the first city builder, Cain, who was also the first murderer. Nimrod, "a mighty hunter before the Lord" (a peculiarly ambiguous title), was also famous for building cities, which in turn became the basis for empires (Gen. 10:8–12). When humanity rebelled against God in organized fashion, it was to "build ourselves a city, and a tower with its top in the heavens," rather than being scattered abroad over the face of the earth" (Gen. 11:4). But God was displeased because such settling in would frustrate humanity's move over the earth, and the people were compelled to abandon their city building. Great cities in the Hebrew Scriptures seem often to be symbols of compacted evil: Nineveh, Sodom, Gomorrah, Babylon. It is as if the congesting of people made it easier to forget God or to add to humanity's hubris: "Look at this empire that we have built."

It's hard to find an appreciative word for the city as compared with nature. The Old Testament as a whole rejoices in the wonders of nature, especially in the book of Psalms and also in an extended portion of Job. Those great Hebrew poets saw the wonders of God in nature and found reasons there to adore and worship God. Sometime in the seventeenth century, a folk saying became a proverb: "God made the country, and man made the town." The saying is with us still, but now we've substituted *city* for *town,* because by now a town seems almost countrylike compared to a modern city. Still, the assumption is pervasive that God is more pleased with — or at least more present in — the grass than the asphalt. Is that so?

Here's something that intrigues me and somehow encourages me. While Genesis begins with a negative picture of the city, something strange has happened as the book of Revelation brings the human-divine story to a grand consummation: John the Revelator speaks not of the holy countryside but of the holy *city.* We humans conclude our pilgrimage not by returning to the garden of Eden but by arriving in the city square.

I find this encouraging. It makes me feel that the asphalt is not all bad. At the least, it's not beyond redemption. To the contrary, it's as if the city is where the long, erratic human procession is intended to end. It's quite a city. Since the streets are gold, there are obviously no economic distinctions. There'll be "the river of the water of life, bright as crystal [no pollution!] flowing from the throne of God and of the Lamb through the middle of the street of the city" (Rev. 22:1–2). On either side of the street, the tree of life produces its fruit each month. The leaves of the tree will bring healing to the nations.

That is quite a city.

For now, if we deal responsibly with both the green grass and the asphalt and we remember the creator of everything from soil to iron ore, God will find pleasure. We will be the kind of caretakers God intended us to be.

DAILY PROMISE

Today I will lay a new claim on both grass
and asphalt, asking how I can celebrate
the holy potential in each one.

CHAPTER 22

INTERRUPTIONS

Of all the ordinary things we might hope to redeem by discovering in them God's pleasure, most of us fume more about interruptions than any other element of daily life. How many people say at day's end, "I didn't accomplish anything today. It was just one interruption after another." The complaint is the same across the varieties of life and occupation, whether one is a homemaker, executive, poet, or research scientist. One gets the impression that nearly all the world's problems could be solved if it weren't for life's interruptions.

Perhaps so. As far as I can see, the last time someone worked without interruption was God in the creation story. There was at the outset "a formless void and darkness" (Gen. 1:2), but once God set to work, there was no hint of interruptions. No wonder God could say at regular, happy intervals, "This is good."

On the other hand, God is perhaps the most notable initiator of interruptions. Noah was a good man of no certain occupation when God called him to build a boat. Abraham was apparently happy as an agro-businessman when God interrupted his plans. Moses seems to have settled down to pastoral life when God placed a burning bush in his path. Amos complained that he was minding his own business as a herdsman and dresser of sycamore trees when God made him a prophet. Mary was a happy, betrothed teenager when God's angel disrupted her life. Jesus followed his Father by laying hold of people who were busy with their daily work. The earnest believer and the struggling saint testify that their pursuit of God often is to no gain, when suddenly God chooses to interrupt, as if only then noticing their existence. God is the Great Interrupter.

It's strange, however, that we postmoderns complain about interruptions, since obviously we court them. There was a time when people who wanted to see you came to your home or office in person, often only after having asked permission by a letter or a hand-delivered note. Then came the telephone, by which persons could interrupt at any time, without petition. I remember when many of us said we would accomplish so much more if it weren't for the telephone, but now we carry a cell phone everywhere we go, compulsively checking for new texts and emails as if we are looking to be interrupted. A pastor friend describes herself, ruefully, as "a quivering mass of accessibility." We court interruptions even while complaining that they're the bane of our lives.

The interruption in its most frequent form (and sometimes its most upsetting) is in conversation. You've just launched into your sentence when another person interrupts. Sometimes that person does so with that most illogical statement, "I don't mean to interrupt you, but . . ." and then proceeds to interrupt you. Of course he means to interrupt! That's the whole purpose of his speaking. His apology, if it may be called that, is only a justification for interrupting, a tacit request for you not to be upset by what he's doing. Sometimes, of course, an interruption is called for when the speaker has turned a conversation into a monologue—or worse, a lecture. Rather early in life, most of us learn to put aside all training in courtesy and join the company of interrupters, else in some settings we'll lose any chance of being heard.

The life of interruptions has made practicing skeptics of most of us. When someone asks, "Can I have a minute of your time?" we've learned that the measure of time is almost surely irrelevant. A *minute?* Certainly not of the sixty-second kind. Often, of course, the one receiving the request is also the one who extends the time beyond the original request. Such is the nature of interruptions. We may hate them, but once we've accepted them, we tend to add substantially to their duration and dominion.

However, fret as we will about interruptions, we nevertheless inflict our interruptions on others (though sometimes guiltily), and we often find that the interruption is better than whatever it broke into. This shouldn't entirely surprise us, because as we read the story of Jesus, we discover that his ministry and miracles could well be organized around interruptions.

Jesus' daily travels were more interruptions than planned events. No wonder—the world then, as now, was filled with people in need, and such people discovered that whatever their need, Jesus could do for them what others could not. Whether they were seeking bodily healing, deliverance from tortured minds, or answers to questions large and small, Jesus was able. So if he was walking purposefully to another town, or in conversation with his disciples, or on his way to help a grieving family, people interrupted him. They had needs, and their needs compelled them.

There was Bartimaeus the blind beggar. He was loud, and the people who tried to silence him were even louder. Nevertheless, Jesus paused in his journey to allow the poor man to explain his interruption, and then Jesus justified the interruption by granting the request. And the woman with an issue of blood was timid, so she tried to avoid an outright interruption. No matter—Jesus himself saw to it that it became a full-scale interruption, and he blessed it.

Some of Jesus' most significant conversations began with interruptions. Most of us will say that this is rarely the case in our experience with interruptions, but it does happen. Of course, if we had more of Jesus' ability to cope with human problems, our interruptions would more often have happy endings.

Many years ago, before there were cell phones, I was becoming increasingly frustrated by the telephone. I was the pastor of a rather large church. I was cautious about cutting myself off from people; I feared that if I made myself unavailable, I might unintentionally turn aside the persons most in need. I didn't like the inner irritation that was developing in my spirit each time I received a call.

Then one day I received counsel from a godlier soul. He had taped a message on his telephone so that each time he picked up the receiver he would see it: "I am about to talk with a child of God." The message told me the most important thing I needed to know about any call that would come my way, a fact more basic than the person's specific need or assumed level of importance or lack thereof. The person on the other end of the line was somebody in whom God had a stake, a person for whom Christ died. Whatever else I might think, I must begin with this ultimate fact. And I must end there too.

I also reminded myself that this person with whom I was about to talk might not know that he was a child of God. There might be no opportunity in this particular call to persuade him of that fact, but I wanted to be sure, at the least, that I didn't make him feel less important than he already felt. I am much impressed with Paul's philosophy that in the fields of eternity, one person sows the seed, another waters it, and God gives the increase. I reason that each human relationship, whether brief or extended, whether deep or apparently superficial, may be part of the Spirit's sowing and nurturing process. I am always a contributor or a deterrent in the fields of God—especially when it comes to interruptions.

So how do we judge which interruptions are the God-pleasing kind and which are merely temptations to distract us from important work at hand? Clearly all interruptions are not created equal. Jesus made rather short shrift of some interrupters, including some who were volunteering their services. Some people, by the nature of their own lives, have no idea what it is to be busy. Others have no sense of time. (Introductory statements such as "All I need is about five minutes" are typically a warning signal.) I'm afraid, too, that there are persons whose ego is such that they feel they deserve attention above anyone else; they move to the front of every line, expect an immediate response to emails or calls, consider their table the only one in a crowded restaurant.

I have no infallible rule for judging interruptions. I know that by accepting one person's interruption I may very well be pushing aside another person. I know still further that I may be unfair in judgment because some interrupters appeal to me more than others.

With all of that, I remind myself that God is the first of the interrupters and that God may be present even in an apparently ungodly interruption. It would be quite dreadful to miss the purposes of God by my impatience with interruptions. So I keep reminding myself that, whatever the interruption, I can give pleasure to God by the graciousness of my coping. God, the Great Interrupter, may be in this interruption.

DAILY PROMISE

Today I will see each interruption as a possible
occasion of eternal significance, because it is.

CHAPTER 23

THE SUM OF IT ALL

This book has traveled down several of life's common roads: roads as ordinary as eating, sleeping, and working. The roads have overlapped at times, as common roads will; this is a tribute to their importance and their commonness. If you had drawn up the journey, you would probably have added some and eliminated others. I make no claim to a complete list or a perfect one. I've worked with two criteria: that the roads would be common to most people and that our celebration of the ordinary could possibly bring God pleasure.

Life is made up almost entirely of routine matters. We call them ordinary because we experience them not by choice but because they are *there*. But my faith insists that nothing is common simply because it is always present. Take the heartbeat for instance—that most present, frequent, and ignored activity unless it becomes irregular or absent. We know, common as it is, that that incessant beat is our ultimate, personal miracle. And there's God, even more present than the heartbeat, yet whose presence we're likely to recognize only at spare or demanding moments.

I want to bring this common life close to our walk with God. Classical theology teaches that God is omniscient (all-knowing) and omnipresent (always with us). If God is indeed with us at all times, God knows us in our common pursuits, since that's how we spend most of our time. Yet this is the void in so much of our religious experience. We're inclined to think upon God primarily in life's extraordinary moments—those especially beautiful times that elicit our thanks or the most trying times, when we seek God's help.

Jesus pictured God as attentive to the fall of a sparrow and as interested in us to such an extent that God has numbered the hairs on our heads. The psalmist communicated the same idea: "You know when I sit down and / when I rise up; / you discern my thoughts from far away, / you search out my path and my lying down, / and are acquainted with all my ways" (Ps. 139:2–3).

These are sublime pictures of God, disarming in their simplicity. They show the vastness of God's knowledge, but far more important, the quality of God's love: a love that finds pleasure in the common stuff of our lives (our "lying down" and "all my ways"), which surely includes both our red-letter days and our ordinary ones.

It is this vision of God that I commend for the ordinariness of our common days. I believe that in such a life perspective and practice, we bring a smile of pleasure to God.

This language will offend some. True, it leans to the childlike, sentimental side. For a rigidly reverent person, it is a little too cozy.

I'm struck, however, by another factor: that such a life is difficult to attain. Most of us have rare moments when we experience some holy epiphany: lunchtime with a friend or loved one that becomes a sacrament, or a walk at sunset that feels like Eden before we spoiled it. But it hardly occurs to us to find God in the average day at work, the hours of reorganizing our files or the implements in our garage, or the all-too-routine conversation, and to think that in such common territory as these we might evoke a divine smile. We calculate that such an outlook is for the saints.

Exactly! That's the sum of it all, and that's where we come in. The influential French novelist Leon Bloy (1846–1917), for years an atheist and then a passionate believer, insisted that the only real failure is not to be a saint, for the pursuit of holiness in all we do is our highest calling. Saintliness is not for clergy, theologians, and church officials (though they're as welcome as anyone). The door to godly living is much wider than we are willing to recognize (many of us happily exempt ourselves by declaring that this must be a very select group) but also much narrower than is expected by those who think God's abundant love means that God has no standards.

The Eric Liddell story, assisted by Saint Paul, has instructed my thinking. Like millions of others, I am captured by Liddell's statement that God had made him *fast* and that when he ran, he felt God's pleasure. If these were not Liddell's actual words, they surely reflected his way of living.

But regardless of their beauty, Liddell's words seemed somehow exclusive. It was fine for an Olympic champion to feel that God took pleasure in his speed, but what about those of us who win few if any races of any kind? How can a discerning God delight in us? This is where a first-century Olympic fan, Paul, helps. Writing to an ordinary body of believers in ancient Corinth, he reminded them that "in a race the runners all compete, but only one receives the prize." He urged his followers in the Way so to compete that they would never "run aimlessly" but would expect to win the prize—because obviously God hopes for all in the Way to win the "imperishable" wreath (1 Cor. 9:24–26). We don't have to be fast, as the culture judges it, but we need to compete with passion—not to defeat others but to fulfill our own holy potential.

That is, the "average believer" should become a champion in daily living. Our racetrack is common, of course, because life itself is common. It is a world of eating and sleeping, of working, reading, learning, moving, and commuting. We play it out in the sometimes tedious settings of relationships and interruptions. We do some of it in green places that remind us of Eden, but the places in other moments — more of them, probably — look like a world that Cain and Nimrod built.

Some see the possibilities better than others. When Flannery O'Connor was only twenty or twenty-one but already at work on her novel *Wise Blood*, she confided to God in her journal, "There's a whole sensible world around me that I should be able to turn to your praise, but I cannot do it." But then she realized how at times it happens: "Yet at some insipid moment when I may possibly be thinking of floor wax or pigeon eggs, the opening of a beautiful prayer may come up from my subconscious and lead me to write something exalted."[1] In her earnest spiritual struggles, she had stumbled on the secret: God is here, in our common places, even our "insipid moments" — verily, in the midst of floor wax and pigeon eggs. While we look for God in philosophy, science, and theology, God waits for us in our common life, our daily minutiae.

Phyllis McGinley won the Pulitzer Prize for poetry in 1961. Along the way, she wrote a delightful book on the saints (*Saint-Watching*), primarily those identified by her own Roman Catholic tradition but including also people like Florence Nightingale and John Wesley. She confessed at the outset that when she was seven years old, she wanted to be a tightrope dancer, at twelve an international spy, and at fifteen a stage actor. "Now in my sensible or declining years," she continued, "I would give anything (except my comforts, my customs, and my sins) to be a saint."[2]

I smiled as I read her words and still more as I read the description of her on the book jacket: "one of America's most beloved poets and chroniclers of the challenges and felicities of ordinary living." "Just the right stuff for a saint!" I said to myself. For it is in the "challenge and felicities of ordinary living" that we have the most opportunities to honor Christ, to bless our fellow creatures and the world God has created, and to get a right estimate of ourselves. Where better to glorify God than in a night's rest, while bathing or shaving, at the breakfast table, approaching a traffic light at a crowded intersection, or reading the morning paper or email? Good things can easily be made evil by our misuse. The aim, thus, of this book is that we take life's common stuff and live it to God's pleasure. Then it won't go wrong.

When the church was very young, the Greek theologian Irenaeus (c. 130–200) wrote, "The glory of God is the person fully alive." I find the same mood in a hymn Isaac Watts wrote in 1707 ("Marching to Zion") but that Robert Lowry's tune made into a rollicking gospel song 160 years later: "The hill of Zion yields a thousand sacred sweets / before we reach the heavenly fields, / or walk the golden streets."[3]

Perhaps that's something of what John the Revelator meant when he said that in heaven, time will be filled with the adoration of God — not that we'll be singing hymns and praying constantly but that whatever occupies us will give God pleasure. If so, it seems a good idea to begin now.

DAILY PROMISE

Today I will be a champion in living. I
will run my race for all its eternal worth,
expecting to see God's smile of pleasure.

NOTES

Chapter 1: The Pleasure of God: A Way of Life

1. Catherine Swift, *Eric Liddell* (Minneapolis: Bethany House Publishers, 1990), 79.

2. Gilbert Keith Chesterton, "The Notebook," in *The Collected Works of G. K. Chesterton* (San Francisco: Ignatius Press, 1994), 43.

Chapter 2: Eating

1. Conrad Aiken, "Discordants," in *Turns and Movies and Other Tales in Verse* (Boston: Houghton Mifflin Company, 1916), 24.

2. Joshua Sundquist, *Daily Guideposts 2014* (New York: Guideposts, 2013), 59.

3. Jenny Schroedel, *The Everything Saints Book*, 2nd ed. (Avon: Adams Media, 2001), 68.

Chapter 6: Working

1. Madeleine L'Engle, *The Rock That Is Higher* (Wheaton: Harold Shaw Publishers, 1993), 122.

2. Charles Hutchinson Gabriel, "When He Comes," in *The Singers and Their Songs: Sketchers of Living Gospel Hymn Writers* (Chicago: The Rodeheaver Company, 1916), 31.

Chapter 7: Cleanliness

1. Joseph L. Baron, *A Treasury of Jewish Quotations* (Lanham: Rowman & Littlefield Publishers, 1985), 55.
2. Ibid.
3. Quoted in Menachem M. Brayer, *The Jewish Woman in Rabbinical Literature: A Psychosocial Perspective* (Jersey City: KTAV Publishing House, 1986), 270.

Chapter 8: Conversation

1. Lady Holland, *A Memoir of the Reverend Sydney Smith, Vol. 1* (London: Longman, Brown, Green and Longmans, 1855), 366.
2. John Emory, *The Works of the Reverend John Wesley, A.M., Vol. VI* (New York: J. Emory and B. Waugh, 1831), 523.

Chapter 11: Relationships

1. Michael Ellison, "Only the Lonely," *The Guardian Weekend*, June 5, 1999, 27.
2. Henry W. Longfellow, "Tales of a Wayside Inn," in *The Complete Poetical Works of Henry Wadsworth Longfellow* (Oxford: Benediction Classics, 2011), 508.
3. John Donne, "No Man Is an Island," in *The Works of John Donne*, vol. 3 (London: John W. Parker, 1839), 574–75.
4. C. S. Lewis, *The Weight of Glory and Other Addresses* (New York: Macmillan, 1949), 15.

Chapter 12: Playing

1. Robert Louis Stevenson, "Happy Thought," in *The Complete Poetry of Robert Louis Stevenson* (Digireads.com, 2011), 23.
2. G. K. Chesterton, "Oxford from Without," in *All Things Considered*, quoted in *The International Thesaurus of Quotations* (New York: Thomas Y. Crowell, 1970), 475.

Chapter 14: Moving

1. Isaac Watts, "Marching to Zion," in *The United Methodist Hymnal* (Nashville: The United Methodist Publishing House, 1989), 733.

Chapter 15: Entertainment

1. Neil Postman, foreword to *Amusing Ourselves to Death* (New York: Penguin Books, 1986), vii.

Chapter 16: Learning

1. Joseph L. Baron, *A Treasury of Jewish Quotations* (Lanham: Rowman & Littlefield Publishers, 1985), 272.
2. Quoted in Roy B. Zuck, *The Speaker's Quote Book* (Grand Rapids: Kregel Publications, 1997), 300.
3. Basil William Miller, *George Washington Carver, God's Ebony Scientist* (Grand Rapids: Zondervan Publishing House, 1943), 118.

Chapter 17: Solitude

1. Vladimir Nabokov, *Pale Fire* (New York: Random House, 1989), 95.
2. Octavio Paz, *The Labyrinth of Solitude* (New York: Grove Press, 1985), 195.
3. Laurie Haller, *Recess: Rediscovering Play and Purpose* (Canton: The Cass Community Publishing House, 2015), 205.

Chapter 18: Walking

1. John Updike, *Self-Consciousness* (New York: Random House, 2012), 244, 255.

Chapter 19: Reading

1. Larry Witham, *A City upon a Hill* (New York: HarperOne, 2007), 23.
2. Joseph Brodsky, quoted in Sven Birkerts, *The Gutenberg Elegies* (Boston: Faber & Faber, 1994), 13.

Chapter 20: Shopping

1. Ruth Styles, "Brits Spend 18 Full Days a Year Trudging Round the Shops," *DailyMail.com*, March 18, 2013, http://www.dailymail.co.uk/femail/article-2295244 /Brits-spend-18-days-year-shopping.html.

2. News Guy, "Average American Spends a Whole Week Every Year Shopping," Financial Press Gazette, December 1, 2010, http://financialpressgazette.com/average-american -spends-a-whole-week-every-year-shopping/.

3. Joshua Becker, "9 Reasons Buying Stuff Won't Make You Happy," becomingminimalist, http://www.becoming minimalist.com/buying-stuff-wont-make-you-happy/.

4. "UPS Pulse of the Online Shopper: A Customer Experience Survey" (white paper, UPSP, June 2014), 4, https://www.ups.com/media/en/2014-UPS-Pulse-of-the -Online-Shopper.pdf.

Chapter 21: Green Grass and Asphalt

1. Joyce Kilmer, "Trees," in *Trees and Other Poems* (Lenox: HardPress, 2008), 19.

2. Linell Nash Smith, "Song of the Open Road," in *The Best of Ogden Nash* (Lanham: Ivan R. Dee, 2007), 72.

3. T. S. Elliot, "Choruses from the Rock," in *T. S. Elliot: Collected Poems, 1909–1962* (San Diego: Harcourt Brace Jovanovich, 1968), 154.

4. Gerard Manley Hopkins and Catherine Phillips, "God's Grandeur," in *Gerard Manley Hopkins: The Major Works* (Oxford: Oxford University Press, 2009), 128.

5. Ibid., 128.

Chapter 23: The Sum of It All

1. Flannery O'Connor, *A Prayer Journal* (New York: Farrar, Straus & Giroux, 2013), 7.

2. Phyllis McGinley, *Saint-Watching* (New York: Viking Press, 1969), 3.

3. Isaac Watts, "Marching to Zion," in *The United Methodist Hymnal* (Nashville: The United Methodist Publishing House, 1989), 733.

CPSIA information can be obtained
at www.ICGtesting.com
Printed in the USA
FFOW03n1157040516
23780FF